The Culture of Ethics

The Culture of Ethics

Franco La Cecla and Piero Zanini

Translated by Lydia G. Cochrane

PRICKLY PARADIGM PRESS
CHICAGO

Prickly Paradigm Press, LLC
5629 South University Avenue
Chicago, Il 60637

www.prickly-paradigm.com

ISBN: 9780984201044
LCCN: 2013952225

Printed in the United States of America on acid-free paper.

Contents

1
It Happens When You Travel

"But let's begin at the top: you, do you have moral principles?"

"Principles, not exactly, I think; maybe I have the scruples of morality."

Tommaso Landolfi, *A Caso*

Anyone who travels knows well that a portion of our attention, when we arrive in a place that is new to us, is focused on understanding how daily life works in the city or the country in which we find ourselves. The Italian proverb "Paese che vai usanze che trovi" (literally, The country you go to, the customs you find) means that one soon learns to conform to another rhythm of life and other ways of thinking about times of day and the spaces devoted to personal matters or life in common. To travel is to want to go toward a constant discontinuity that continually forces you to position yourself and deal, step by step, with the habits of others. This seems almost like a contradiction, because we think of travel as a way to escape daily life, yet the first thing that we do when we find ourselves in a country that is different from our own is to learn (or re-learn) the local rhythms and the local daily routine.

In Hanoi in the morning breakfast is a *phò* soup accompanied by a yeast bread shaped like a Spanish *churro*. To be sure, if you stay in your hotel this will never happen to you, but if you begin to stroll around and mix with the locals, at a certain point you will understand how important it is to begin the day with what the Vietnamese consider the quintessential meal.

If you live in Spain for a while, you will find yourself, as an outsider, wondering why the cities are empty, deserted from two to five in the afternoon, and as long as you fail to understand that this respite allows the day to be prolonged until past nightfall you will not have grasped one of the laws of daily life in Spain.

All countries have a moment when time is suspended: bar time in Rome, the time of the *ginjinha* in Lisbon, that of a *demi* of beer in a French bistro, or the pause for *chai* in a Turkish café near the port. Such suspensions of time are more important than continuities for setting the rhythm of daily life; they give a sense of beginning, of the passage from one phase to another during the day, of coming toward evening, and of the end of the day.

Every culture has invented ways and rituals for giving daily rhythms a sense of an "exceptional normality," from the little old ladies reciting vespers in a Sicilian village to the five daily prayers of Islam or the Hindu *puja* accompanied by a little bell to chase away spirits and awaken consciousness. But ritual behavior can also be the time to buy a *durian* in the open markets of Bangkok or that of waiting for a group *camioneta* in the periphery of Quito.

If you walk along the streets of the "French concession" in Shanghai, you will realize how many suspensions and how many rhythms people use to "kill" time, from participating in animated discussions in front of a display of fish in a market to playing *mah-jong* or setting linens out to dry along the *lilong*, the alleys between the low houses of this part of the city.

Anyone who travels might well wonder what these habits are, why they are so important, and why they differ so from one land to another. They are different, yet they all take us back to one question: that of "knowing" what to do with one's own daily life. Rather, they *are* daily life; they are the scansions that allow experience to be different from an indistinct flow of time. The discontinuity that they create becomes a tenuous but constant form of rule and of rules. These are not directly rules of good and bad, even if this form of "know-how" and of the art of living is the substratum, the rug woven day by day onto which every other form of morality can be embroidered.

Such is the "ordinary" ethics that we need for everyday living and for knowing "how to get along" with those who live next to us. It is a form of conformity that demands an apprenticeship, followed by a near forgetting of that apprenticeship. Foreigners, travelers, and external observers are the ones who realize that people, in one place or another, "give themselves rules" and, in most cases, tacitly respect them. These rules are for living well, for agreement or for litigation. They are rules for the common use of spaces; they are norms of "manners" that can also become norms of "sincerity" or "authenticity"; they are what the anthropologists have called "culture," thus implying that these banal daily norms hide the meaning that people give to their own lives.

Within these rules there are also scruples, awkwardness, and shifts of position, precisely because between individuals and the community in any given location there is a continual interplay of conformity and non-conformity. Adolescents, for example, play at testing adult rules, and often single individuals feel constrained by those same rules, which at times they help—with great difficulty—to change. Anyone who does not conform is pushed out of play and is himself disturbed by his own imperfect conformity, but, what is more, he disturbs the majority that surrounds him with his discordant voice. Daily ethics is a "drift" that moves more slowly than individuals and carries them along like a slow current that some resist by swimming in another direction.

Clifford Geertz tells us in *The Interpretation of Cultures* that culture consists in structures of a socially established significance, adding that culture is public because meaning is. Those structures are the ones that resist us when we travel; those into which we must at least partially attempt to enter if we do not want to close ourselves up inside the inn or the hotel. They are resistant, because they are thick and deep and they range from the rhythms and scansions of daily life as far as lifetime events, birth, emotions, fears, pain and joy, belonging (or not) to a masculine or feminine world, the sense of being together and of being alone, the ages of life, the meaning of doing and speaking, the death of others and one's own death. They require "thick description" because they are the result of a history and of the interaction between that history with a specific place (what elsewhere we have called *mente locale* or "local mind"); because they are the result of a context and of how both history and context have changed. For this reason as well, "they resist us" (that is, such structures resist both we travelers and those who live within them). For this reason, we need a certain lapse of time to enter into them or come out of them.

We should not think that such rules are fixed, or that people are so mired within them that they cannot adjust to new happenings. There is in these daily norms not only the elasticity it takes to fit into the world, but also a dynamic rush toward the future. Or, rather than a "rush," there are profound drifts, tectonic faults that move within the least conscious part of individuals and collectivities.

The anthropologists know by professional deformation that cultures are not "assimilable" and that one cannot attempt to persuade a culture to conform to another or to change except by means of a long process that contains violent traumas or follows disastrous or extraordinary happenings. But culture "resists," and one of its characteristics is precisely that of being suspended between the drifting currents of daily life—things that people do "normally," no longer asking themselves why—and an even deeper and unconscious structure, that of dreams and of the subterranean drifts that entire throngs and populations keep within themselves without knowing it.

Some have spoken of "sleepwalking," or a form of suggestion that permeates the "I" that discovers itself in interaction with the body social. This is a reflection that Gabriel Tarde made in 1884 in an article titled "Qu'est-ce qu'une société?" As Andrea Cavalletti summarizes Tarde's thoughts in an afterword to a recent version of this article in Italian:

> At base there is therefore a knowing-how-to-be that is at once birth, growth, affirmation and dispersion of the "I" in a myriad of relations that are always new. There is always a social body, a place of mind-to-mind transmission, a body or an echo of ideas, and underneath that body, the first capture. There is,

in fact, in principle a relationship of possession or fascination exerted by that singular object that resists our glance, while it strikes us in virtue of its force as a subject. Because that redoubling on the basis of which, seeing the other, I discover myself would not be what it is (would not give any awareness of itself) if it did not implicate an "irresistible faith" in the reality of the other consciousness. Looking at a flower, a mountain, a tree, Tarde says, I can forget myself, lose myself completely in what I see. This is not true when I look at a man ("or even a superior animal"): I cannot see him without telling myself that the other will be equally empowered to look at me. And I am already in his power.

This state is not a closed or static sleepwalking, but rather an abandonment of the self where the imitation and the suggestion in which individual and society are united become a desiring dynamic. Individual and society are immersed in an "ordinary" ethics that seems absolutely stable, precisely because it moves slowly, imperceptibly, and drags everything along with it.

That suspension between a daytime daily life that seems immobile and a subterranean daily life has a resistance and a friction that give the culture to which one belongs the appearance of being the only reality. To be realists demands that we not forget that if we go elsewhere, to another land, the principles of realism change.

Cultures are diverse, but given their thickness and the fact that they are structures of meaning, each one of them claims to be the principle of reality, the actual truth to be taken seriously and to which one must conform or rebel against. Cultures manifest their own reasons for being with extreme conviction, and if listened to from the inside these reasons seem incontrovertible.

2

The Rules for Doing Nothing

Life has no parts, but faces and places.
Maria Zambrano, *Claros del bosque*

Two Swedish anthropologists, Billy Ehn and Orvar Löfgren, have written a book on "doing nothing" that is an account of the ways in which people occupy their daily lives with activities that seem irrelevant, but that constitute its true substratum. They distinguish three categories of activities in their "doing nothing."

The first of these are routines: what people do out of habit: alimentary habits and those related to dress and speaking, including pat phrases and gestures; habits that can be experienced as reassuring or oppressing, but that in all cases reoccur in daily life, making it a sort of constant repetition and warding off the anguish of emptiness, of the unusual, and of the eruption of the unexpected in life.

Having routines can make the flow of time very sweet, relating it to the recurrent shifts of day and night, the cycle of the seasons, and changes in plants and flowers. At times there is nothing better than to give oneself over to the certainty of such recurrences, in which culture becomes for a moment nature and pretends that it, too, is a part of the cycles and the seasons. Routines are what save us in difficult moments, and permit us to live through personal and collective dramas, epochal crises, and transformations in the world. They are what enable us to feel that "life goes on."

Philosophy and sociology have been cognizant of these repetitive structures and have given them different names, ranging from the "forms of life" of Ludwig Wittgenstein to the "techniques of the body" of Marcel Mauss, the "habitus" of Pierre Bourdieu, and the "ordinary" morality that Stanley Cavell speaks of, re-elaborating Wittgenstein, up to and including what Peter Sloterdjiek calls "daily athletics," or the athletics of repetition. Simply by repeating gestures, words, and actions, these structures become part of us, and at the same time they are a training that permits us to transform our bodies and our minds, rendering us capable of being at ease in the society that surrounds us. They are a good part of what we have defined elsewhere (Franco La Cecla, *Saperci fare: Corpi e autenticità*) as a "nonchalance," an ability to be at ease in everyday actions, practices, and manners.

That nonchalance represents something like a craft: we learn "how to do things" just as we learn "how to become ourselves"—that is, how to be sympathetic, sociable, seductive, convincing—and just as we learn to seem to be expert, courageous, competent, or someone who "knows his trade." It is the same for places. The business of living in them requires an ability to orient oneself, to use available resources, to be part of those resources and be capable of using them as a point of departure for our own experiences in the world.

The quotidian is not spontaneous: it is the least spontaneous thing there is. To the point that if you ask a population why it does the things that it does, day after day, the only response you will get is "because they have always been done this way." The body, individual or collective, absorbs the lessons that it forgets in the repetition of gestures. It becomes a competent body, but it does not really know why it has become natural to do or not do certain things. The "techniques of the body" that Marcel Mauss speaks of, but also Claude Lévi-Strauss's "homme bricoleur" belong within the same sort of unconscious competences. We do not need to learn, time after time, to move ourselves, to drive a car, to walk in a certain way, to sleep according to certain rhythms, to seduce, to know how to hold a conversation, to cook, to feed our children, to tell stories, to distinguish resources for daily life in a forest or in a city.

The second category defined by the Swedish anthropologists is waiting. Daily life is broken up by continual expectations. In part these are bodily expectations—hunger, thirst, desire, sleep—and in part they are made up by waiting for a bus, awaiting one's turn at the post office, standing in line to buy something, waiting for the children to get out of school, waiting for the rain, the sun, or waiting for a shower to be over; waiting for someone; waiting for the birth of a child. These waits and expectations are slow movements of time, moments in which it seems that time is slower than we are, and that we have to follow its lead in order to be able to wait.

Waiting, as the much-missed Wislawa Szymborska tells us, occurs in situations in which the soul is sometimes not present:

We have a soul at times.
No one's got it non-stop,
for keeps.

Day after day,
year after year,
may pass without it.
. . .
It rarely lends us a hand
in uphill tasks,
like moving furniture,
or lifting luggage,
Or going miles in shoes that pinch.

It usually steps out
whenever meat needs chopping
or forms have to be filed.
. . .
Joy and sorrow
aren't two different feelings for it.
It attends us
only when the two are joined.

We can count on it
when we're sure of nothing
and curious about everything.
. . .
We need it
but apparently
it needs us
for some reason too.

The soul is not present during periods of waiting because we have to confound it with the time that
obliges us to become passive, to make us be carried
along by its slow, even too slow, flow.

There are collective waiting periods, times of
patience and resistance, that require the hope that

things can change. There is what James C. Scott calls "the arts of resistance." There is what lies behind official history and that creates the subterranean and patient capacity to make spaces of opposition, as now in China where it is the social networks that are forming a basic network of commentary and diversity within the new word of the party in power, which invites all to make money and consume goods but prevents any form of meeting, gathering, or discussion in public places. These are the waiting periods in which new identities are made, those shifts dear to anthropologists, who know that cultures are not swept away in the blink of an eye, but resist, go underground and eventually, when they can do so, reemerge transformed, in part or in whole.

Finally, the third category that Ehn and Löfgren propose is daydreaming, that of Tarde's sleepwalking or Benjamin's dreams with one's eyes wide open. People, crowds, what was once called the masses, populations, entire tribes, and entire communities settled in the crowded slums of Mumbai or Caracas dream with their eyes open or closed. Dharawi, a slum of Mumbai often depicted in Indian films, dreams of a world that somewhat resembles that of Bollywood, with its heroes and heroines, but it also dreams of other possible worlds. It is those dreams that move the tectonic plates of history, that push what historians call "mentalities" toward a transformation; that make the truth that people search in their own lives something that is going to be made actual thanks to a tension borne by an entire city and by an entire community. This is the category of archeology of the present that concerns Michel Foucault and that has been related so sublimely by Walter Benjamin.

Benjamin—especially in his texts regarding Paris as the capital city of the nineteenth century—intuits that the collectivity is transported by oneiric currents in which city spaces play a fundamental role. Cities are spaces within which the city population's dreams (with eyes open or closed) become visible and find concrete forms, as was the case with the *passages* of Paris at the end of the nineteenth century. Societies move forward through these experiences. Entire crowds make use of the city in which they live as a space for their own dreams, projecting onto it, exactly as if on a cinema screen, their own collective desires. There are experiences of entire generations that underlie movements that lead to the dizzying peaks of modernity; to the attraction for the illusion of the cinema; to the temptation of ubiquity; to the will to free oneself from oppressive political and social structures; to profound fears that push people into the hands of worse powers; to dreams of wealth and of equality; and to dreams of redemption and palingenesis. The cinema, the media, and speed have been the dreams of Western culture for over a century, and today they make way for other currents, those of a world felt to be totally reachable, or, to the contrary, those of a localism experienced as defense, or even the dream of eternal company—the media are always with us—and that of the most extreme individualism.

This is what we can intuit watching the documentary *Tahrir: Liberation Square* (2012), by Stefano Savona, which tells the story of Tahrir Square in Cairo, a protagonist in the long (and continuing) Egyptian revolution. It was being in the square, in the space where people camped and resisted Mubarak's police forces, that finally gave discontent with a regime the solid flesh that enabled it to become a city and to transform dreams into possibilities. What was previously whispered fearfully now is a collection of faces in a specific place. It was in that square that what had been a clandestine dream became a face-to-face encounter between different groups who finally could speak openly as they never would have dared to do before the "invention" of Tahrir Square as a place of redemption.

In this process of being close together, in imitation of bodily entities and their mutual suggestion, routines and daily expectations are carried on underground by the eroticism of the social connection, which is also, as Benjamin has taught us, an eroticism "apparently" moved over to merchandise. The squares and the streets of the cities are marketplaces that put into act collective desires, as a representation of collective life that can become an exchange, a project, and a hope. If the oneiric aspect of cities and their daily life is not understood, the behavior of the crowd can appear to be absurd and inexplicable. It is the eroticism of the social space that makes places like the *grands magasins parisiens* so beloved by the crowd. One of the characteristics of daily life is precisely that relationship with merchandise, along with its becoming animate, as if things were persons. The fetishism of merchandise, which Marx intuited but was truly excavated only by Benjamin, means that merchandise is erotic because the life and the exchange that people make of it becomes attached to it. Things, objects in a store window, are alive and become part of society and of the exchanges of desires that take place in everyday life.

The daydreaming of the peasant who now lives in Peking or Hanoi is in part frustrating and in part is a substitution for the desire that has to circulate in a society in order for it to feel the movement that spurs on daily life. Desire is social desire, the desire of bodies present together in the public spaces of the city. Merchandise is simply an intermediary.

Benjamin insists on the dialectic between collective dream and being awake, on the oneiric currents that sink and reemerge, and that have for him something to do with the messianism of which he was convinced and with the desire for liberation that pushes history forward. The messianic key explains in what manner the ordinary "hatches" the future; in what manner its seeds are kept warm by those open-eyed dreams that Benjamin discovered in the collective imaginary. That profound river that runs under history—the profound current of daily daydreaming—keeps moving until it "runs into" something, and when that happens the tectonic faults rise up, new continents emerge, and others sink.

3

Other People's Rules

A novel of Mischa Berlinski's, *Fieldwork*, tells an exemplary story. It concerns a female American anthropologist who goes to a Dyalo village on the border between Burma (now Myanmar) and Thailand to do fieldwork. The Dyalo do not really exist, but they resemble other tribes that do live in the zone: they have a language that uses eight tones and is hard to master and a complex cosmology linked to the cultivation of rice. When two Dyalo meet, they inquire about the other's health by asking, "Is your rice happy?" The anthropologist seeks to understand whatever there is to understand: the structure of kinship, languages, myths, stories, ways of establishing a relationship with resources and with the ancestors. It is a long and difficult task. "In the field" she meets a dynasty of missionaries who follow the same tribe, know its language, its customs, and the underlying structures of daily life, and for three generations have been working to convert its members. After a year or two the anthropologist returns to the United States to finish her doctoral thesis, and despite the trials she went through when she was with the tribe, a profound nostalgia pushes her to request a scholarship to return there for a longer stay. She obtains the grant and finds herself back in the field, more convinced than ever of the importance of the culture that she has been studying, and in particular its extraordinary, almost erotic relationship with the rice fields, the seasons, and the landscape. She knows the shaman, and a strong connection—a passion—is established between them that adds to her enthusiasm for anthropology. In short, she feels herself more and more a part of a culture whose beauty and motivations she feels she understands. In the meantime, the missionaries continue to operate, in particular the youngest member of the dynasty, who, after undergoing a serious crisis, went to live in America for a while but returned to Thailand with renewed faith.

Berlinski tells the story in the form of an investigation that he himself has carried on, beginning from the moment he came to know from a friend that the anthropologist, who had been locked up in a Thailandese prison for having killed the young missionary, has committed suicide. The book—which is fascinating and extremely carefully constructed in its details (the author has lived for years in those parts)—reconstructs the story in the voice of those who have known it well, and it is an outstanding allegory on the principal question of anthropology, which is "Are others, those of other cultures, right?" This might seem a stupid question, but it is the fundamental question that anthropology is called on to respond to and hints of which confront the traveler: The rules that people hold up for themselves in this culture that I am visiting and in the midst of which I am living, are they moral rules that should be respected as if they were rules valid for everyone? But in that case, what should I think of the fact that if I go elsewhere, within another culture, the same rules are considered infractions or repugnant?

Is it possible to do what the anthropologist does and "root for" another culture, defending it from intrusions from cultures other than its own? But are we sure that they "are right" to the point of leading us to kill someone who seeks to change their motivations (as far as the motivations of amorous passion are confounded here with those of anthropology: the shaman was taken away from her due to his conversion to Christianity)? As the novel is constructed it leaves room for many doubts. If the missionaries seem to be bigots intent on indoctrination, we later discover that in many ways they have deeply understood the Dyalo culture, but they have not mythologized it. Is there not a danger that anthropologists mythologize the cultures they are studying well beyond the ways in which those cultures—which are used to changes and transformations—live the value of their own myths? It is as if the anthropologists constantly ran the risk of essentializing a culture, immobilizing it and tying it down to itself, taking it seriously in a manner that is not that of those who live it on a daily basis. A morality for everyday life means that the rules that people give themselves in order to live are living rules and are not, for the most part, lived like external commandments, but as ways of behaving, life practices, and forms of life that, precisely, can also "conform" to new gains and external happenings.

With time anthropology has become much more cautious and more focused in its study of the way in which entire societies and tribes, faced with a new situation, a crisis, or an overall change, have been capable of transforming themselves and of completely "changing" or "updating" their morality, which means their style of life and their motivations. In their capacity for resistance, cultures also have the characteristic of being much more elastic than they seem, and every complaint bemoaning the "destruction of a culture" fails to take into account effective processes by which people and societies are capable of assimilating change, transforming it, adapting to it, but also adapting the change to themselves.

The problem that the novel poses is apparently that of the contrast between those, like the missionaries, who profess a universal morality and those who instead have their "own morality." The missionaries claim to have a moral verity that is not open to doubt and is valid for all humanity, which must be saved from the shadows of backwardness or sin. It is the Western vision of cultures held to be primitive, barbarous, uncivilized. It is also a vision of democratic progress as something "obligatory" for all the peoples of the world.

Anthropologists have done much to lend relevance to the "relative" worth of every culture. Claude Lévi-Strauss did so in *Race and History*, his declaration to UNESCO against universalistic claims in which he stated that every culture has its truth and its morality, which must be respected within an overall picture of differences in ways of being human, unless that culture breaks certain fundamental moral parameters such as infanticide, violence toward women, infibulation, cannibalism, or general violence against other human groups. From a generalized relativism we have shifted to the conviction that there are universal human rights that cannot be ignored. Also because the claim of Western culture to be the only true culture is shared by every culture and every tribal group convinced that it is the only truly human group.

At this point, the question that the novel poses becomes a bit more complex. It is not a question of universalism and relativism, but rather of the way in which individuals can live the relationship with others' moralities. In the final analysis, the anthropologist is not very different from the missionaries: she too has a missionary intent, a duty that rises within her to work for the salvation of the indigenous people whom she loves.

In recent years anthropology has witnessed the emergence of a sizeable interest in "applied anthropology." Here anthropologists are not only called on to study and observe without intervening, but they begin to raise questions about how to work to defend the rights of the peoples they study. Even more, they have to accept the fact that their role is challenged: it is precisely the indigenous peoples whom they are studying who should be active in the study of their own culture. The point of view of the natives proposed by anthropology of the late 1980s and by the critical anthropology of George Marcus and Michael Fischer goes in that direction. The point of view of the anthropologist must not do violence to the vision that indigenous populations have of themselves.

Experiments such as Survival International, Cultural Survival, and the International Work Group for Indigenous Affairs (IWGIA) have brought about an anthropology "on the side of" the indigenous populations, who are conceived of as the carriers of a cultural richness to be defended and, especially, of an ecological awareness of nature and its resources. It is as if the indigenous peoples were superior to us and more coherent in placing their culture in a correct relationship with nature; as if, in fact, they represented a "state of nature" that we have lost. Obviously, this is not the case, and often it leads to misunderstandings. The human nature of indigenous peoples is shaped by culture, as is our own, and it makes possible a more harmonic relationship with the forest, the desert, the sea, and the river precisely because it has transformed nature into kinship and sees in nature something related to their own society. Indigenous peoples have culturized and socialized nature, while we continue to fool ourselves by thinking that nature exists as an entity apart.

This being said, it is evident that many tribes, indigenous populations, and traditional societies have a deeper and more integrated relationship with their environment—on which they depend and by which they live—and for that reason they must maintain a balanced dialogue with it. That same relationship is put to a harsh test when confronted by capitalist rapacity and the cultural deviation that it brings with it in contexts of the sort—which explains the presence of applied anthropology.

But what should we say of other communities that the anthropologists might study? If, for example, they examine a group of skinheads in the London suburbs, a neo-Nazi group in Scandinavia, or militants of the fundamentalist Hindu party Shiv Sena? What happens when an anthropologist decides to study the Salafi in Muslim lands? In this case, what is applied anthropology? The question of "their" rules and "their" morality obviously arises. Can I, as an anthropologist, share the morality of the fundamentalists or the neo-Nazi groups? Can I share the verbal violence and *machismo* of a rap group from Spanish Harlem in Manhattan? Obviously not. But then, as an anthropologist I am also the bearer of an "outside eye" that makes moral judgments about the moral rules of the group that I am studying.

More generally, a relativist approach to others' moral systems, to their ways of living, and to the culture they share with other groups makes sense up to a certain point. Absolute relativism is a form of absolutism: as Clifford Geertz has explained in magisterial fashion in his classic essay, "Anti Anti-Relativism," the only healthy relativism is a relativist relativism.

4

There's Someone Knocking at the Door

Karen Sykes, who has worked for years among the Mesi, a population of Papua New Guinea, recently found herself in an odd situation. Knocking at her door was Sioni, the son of a "Big Man" who was much-loved and appreciated as head of the tribe. Sioni had come to the door of the anthropologist to ask her help regarding his own son, who was about to "make a bad marriage." She responded, "Why ask me? I don't live here."

The situation was rather complicated, as the anthropologist was well aware. A young woman named Rose was about to be married to Sioni's son, Bartly. Rose, who came from a village on the East Coast of Papua, had met Bartly in the Lihir gold mine in which they both worked. The two agreed to live together, something regarded as very bad in the traditions of both of their villages. Now, accepting the idea of trying remedy the situation and "set it right," Rose wanted to marry Bartly. In this move, which had led Rose to speak with the elders of Bartly's village, there was a strategy that aimed at obtaining for Rose and the future couple the benefits proper to an influential family (which included a house in the village), in addition to those they had acquired as a modern and uninhibited couple. Sioni saw all this as a very calculating move; above all, he was concerned that his son did not understand that matrimony should involve much more than simple cohabitation and an accumulation of advantages.

The anthropologist did not know what to do. Because she was stuck between an awareness of the rules of the village, according to which Rose, when all was said and done, was returning to a respect for traditions, and the legitimate doubts of Bartly's father about the fact that his son was letting himself be led by the nose. Saying "I don't live here" seemed to liberate her from an embarrassing situation. But in fact that was really not true, given that she lived in the village and, as an anthropologist, was well aware of the rules and customs of the Mesi.

> On the one hand, I had fixed my attention so narrowly on customary marriage as being culturally distinct from Western marriage that I imagined him to be living a life very different from my own.... I did not want to discuss his son's marriage because I believed in the incommensurability of his cultural values for a good marriage with mine. I expected Sioni's answer to be coherent with the customary mores of social and cultural life in the village where he and his family lived. This might be error. On the other hand, I was so firmly grounded in my sense of my own rationality and the privileges of that way of

interrogating social life that I felt compelled to analyze how the social relationships should take place, given the deep logic informing them. My commitment to finding the rational reasons for marriage compelled me to ignore the passion of the young woman's plea for Bartly's love, and to focus instead on the logical interest she might have in marriage. The boundaries between her self-interest in the marriage and her interest in Bartly's well-being were difficult to ascertain. If love had anything to do with it, then it was not determinable because the evidence of the quality of that love remained unmeasurable. I tried to answer both with cultural sensitivity and with rational certainty about the nature of the institution of marriage, only to find myself speechless.

This is a typical case of what Sykes herself calls "living paradoxes of a global age." Because, to look at things from the viewpoint of Sioni, he was seeking an answer from the anthropologist precisely because she was an outsider-insider. Since she fell outside the logical system of the village, she could be of genuine help. Sioni had not only broken the seal of anthropological pertinence and the commandment according to which cultures are to be understood within their own logic, but he was using the advantages of a globalized world to seek for aid in a situation of strong transformation of his world. The anthropologist's moral reasoning did not correspond to the moral reasoning of the native, precisely because they had changed roles. The anthropologist continued to look at things from close to hand, while Sioni wanted a more long-range view.

It was for that reason that in recent years anthropology has discovered a new and fascinating world, that of the ethnographies of moral reasons, needed because, in an age of globalization, local moralities and "more universal" moralities do not intersect with one another but often are superimposed on one another, pursue one another, or negate one another. This implies that now more than ever, occupying oneself with anthropology means occupying oneself with people's daily reasoning.

Anthropology is a magnificent source of a new philosophical reflection on the human, precisely because it strives to be faithful to a phenomenology of the human. This is not an abstract and indistinct category; it is the human here, in this precise place, made flesh in men and women, sites, landscapes, communities, ties and relations of kinship and friendship; in histories of generations, street corners, village dust, and fields of rice and grain. Anthropology gives us back the "meat" of the world that philosophy has too long negated. It re-actualizes and transforms the questions of philosophy in a way that is finally concrete: What is morality for the people who live together in a specific place? And what relation is there between this morality and other moralities? How do individuals live out their own morality, and how do they experience collectivities and societies? Is morality what we know from philosophy books as torment before a choice and a judgment? Does it really respond to that fundamental question, "How should I live?" put by Socrates and later picked up by Bernard Williams.

In recent years anthropology has raised these questions, and it is interesting that they are giving rise to a new discipline that is having to redefine a good many basic elements. But it is even more interesting that this new trend is doing so on the basis of case studies and the characteristic anthropological technique of the narration of daily life here and now or in the recent past. Finally, it is the narrative aspect of anthropology that permits it self-interrogation as a privileged discipline regarding ethics and moralities for daily life.

Anthropology's answer to the Socratic question of how to live (and Bernard Williams reminds us that in Greek the question is not personal—not "How should I live?" but "How should one live?") is the "this way" that refers to the way of living that every culture gives itself. To be sure, asking how to live corresponds to a fundamental shift in Greek culture in the age of Socrates, a moment at which formulas for living, faith in the gods, and even faith in the rules of the city had entered into crisis. Socrates takes crisis unto himself, interpreting it and dying of it, thus founding the transition to a manner of living given by the many as solidly established and a new manner that must be sought. Paul K. Feyerabend tells us something similar about a change of paradigm in an even earlier Greek world, when, in the age of the composition of the *Iliad* the behavior of Achilles, who rebels against the normal laws of compensation when his favorite handmaiden is taken away from him, sets off an unexpected crisis situation. The hero was not behaving according to the rules. For Feyerabend, the episode stands for a passage between two different epochal paradigms.

Ignoring the fact that the moral choices of individuals are in continual dialectics with the "formulas for living" that societies give themselves means not understanding that ethics, as "what to do" and "how to live," is a praxis, something that does not concern the individual in his isolated cell and in his heart, but concerns his position in respect to others and, more generally, in how he manages to translate life into living in community.

5
Turbulent Hearts

Unni Wikan, who spent years among the women of Cairo and other years in Bali, an island much studied by anthropologists from Gregory Bateson and Margaret Mead to Clifford Geertz and others, recounts a magnificent example of life in Bali. Almost all scholars agree that Balinese culture is a culture of exteriority, a theater in which the individual and persons do not express their own sentiments, but rather stereotypes of sentiments; a world in which everything seems to have to be always in its place and every peak of expression or emotion must be toned down. Jane Belo, an artist who worked there in the 1930s with Margaret Mead and Gregory Bateson describes that culture: "The babies do not cry, the small boys do not fight, the young girls bear themselves with decorum, the old men dictate with dignity.... The child... has only to obey the prescriptions of tradition to become an adult happily adjusted to the life which is his."

Wikan had a different experience. In a bus that was taking her from the village down to the plain, the anthropologist met a timid young woman, Suriati, who mentions the fact that a person who was a friend of hers had died recently. After a few days the two meet again, and Suriati, still smiling and "bright," tells Wikan than this was in fact a friend who died unexpectedly after an attack of diarrhea. Another few days go by, and eventually the girl confesses that he was a very dear friend, to the point that they were thinking of getting married soon. She also says that she had received a telegram from the family, inviting her to participate in the funeral. The girl was Muslim and the boy was Hindu. Suriati says that she will not go because she does not have the money to travel to his far-away village, and because she must tend to her work in the fields. The following day, still smiling, she asks the anthropologist to help her by lending her money to go to the funeral. Wikan consents, but she is still surprised by the girl's nearly cold emotional response. Suriati disappears, and the anthropologist asks after her among those who know her, who confirm that she indeed left. A few days later she received a letter from the girl, who writes that she could not participate in the funeral because some of her relatives held her back out of fear of the black magic involved in Hindu funerals. The anthropologist suspects that whole story is made up and is afraid that she has put herself in some manner between the family and the girl. But the girl returns, and when Wikan asks her to show her the photograph of the boy, Suriati shows it to her and also shows her photos of herself on his tomb. She says that she cried for two days, until the relatives let her go away. Above all, it had not been easy for her to weep, even if her heart was broken, because when relatives and friends saw her in tears, they said to her, "Well, he is dead. So why do you cry?" and "What's the matter with you, are you crazy!"

Thanks to Suriati, Wikan discovers that the Balinese people feel and suffer just like everyone else in the world, but their system of emotions is a moral system. Given that laughing is considered to do good to oneself and to others, one must always laugh, even in mourning, because it is one way to chase away sadness and malignant spirits and to avoid doing ill to others. Emotions are "feeling-thoughts," Wikan says, that imply a public involvement of oneself with the others. Living in Bali included a "formula for living" in which it was important to "manage turbulent hearts."

Another Balinese friend of Wikan's told her that for the moment she could not leave her mother alone because she would have "no one to laugh with." Laughter was a form of moral commitment, because emotions, contrary to common opinion, are the solid part of the system of daily life in common. This is what explains why we fail to understand in other cultures people's reactions when faced with mourning, sadness, joy, or anxiety. If those facts of life are universal, the sentiments that they bear with them are not necessarily universal. However strange it may seem (at least in the Balinese context), emotions, or "feeling-thoughts," as Robert C. Solomon states, "are regarded as the *choice* and *responsibility* of the person," in the sense that they do not arise from a supposed spontaneity, but rather must be "modeled and chiseled to comply with societal regulations." The fact is:

> Cultural variation in the expressions of affect is one of the most readily observable yet least easily interpretable aspects of human behavior. As a communicative system, affective expression is the inverse of

linguistic expression: while in language the linguistic symbols are considered arbitrary carriers of meaning, affective expression is perceived as embodying meaning itself. We are not surprised when we cannot understand the speech of a person whose language we do not know, but we assume that an adequate translation would convey a meaningful message to us. Observing the affective behavior of a person from a different culture, however, we "know" what is meant, but sometimes are unable to understand why a person should act that way.

In the case of Bali, a moral system of emotions regulates daily life and one's response to life's events, but that does not mean that in private people cannot weep, suffer, or be sad or worried. The Balinese example shows quite well the make-up of a horizontal morality that has to do more with "containment" than with an answer to "How to live?' The response to that question, in Balinese society and in many others, is a question of "style"—what Wikan calls "brightness," a resplendent, sunny, positive way of being that can confront life with dignity and elegance. We shall see below how that behavior leads to an idea of moral rules as aesthetic rules.

6
An Ordinary Ethics

> Instead of the unanalyzable, specific, indefinable: the fact that we act in such-and-such ways, e.g. we *punish* certain actions, *establish* the state of affair[s] thus and so, *give orders*, render accounts, describe colors, take an interest in others' feelings. What has to be accepted, the given—it might be said—are facts of living.
>
> Ludwig Wittgenstein,
> *Remarks on the Philosophy of Psychology*

In Italian, "ordinary" is an adjective that has a slightly negative connotation. Something that is not extraordinary, that is not out of the usual run of things, is ordinary. "Ordinary" refers to something that is without remarkable qualities; that has a prosaic quality that makes it uninteresting. For John L. Austin, the American philosopher and linguist who wrote *How to Do Things with Words*, "ordinary" has a somewhat different meaning. It is within the ordinary rhythms of daily life that we need to search for the linguistic acts that often have a performative efficacy. There are words and phrases "that do things" and that make things happen, and in a life of relations speaking has an efficacy that goes far beyond the exchange of information. Another philosopher, Stanley Cavell, picked up the thoughts of Austin, who, among other things, led him to discover Wittgenstein. In an original synthesis, Cavell reinterprets the idea of the ordinary, filtering it through the thought of Henry David Thoreau and Ralph Waldo Emerson, the two great Americans of the return to evidence, of the celebration of experience, and of the impossibility of reducing experience to thought formulas. Cavell returns to Wittgenstein—who, in his own work had hardly touched on the theme of a personal ethics because he was persuaded that it was impossible to speak of it—and defines the "forms of life" about which Wittgenstein spoke as "criteria" that are in the nature of things and are not imposed conventions.

> Criterial rules... are not externalities, but *internal* to the human form of life. The problem with thinking of criterial rules as conventional is therefore the metaphysically deep one that it misinterprets our relationship to our criteria. It alienates us from them, and thus from ourselves, for our form of life and our criteria are one.

Cavell devotes one of his most important works, *The Claim of Reason*, to the rediscovery of the ordinary (and in fact in Italian translation the book's title is "The Rediscovery of the Ordinary"). Davide Sparti, who edited the Italian translation, observes that the source of this rediscovery is the linguistic question; the call for "what is ordinarily said." Introducing the question of linguistic domination in the daily context, Cavell states:

> In the work of Wittgenstein and Austin... appeals to "what we ordinarily say" take on a different emphasis. In them the emphasis is less on the *ordinariness* of an expression... than the fact that they are *said* (or, of course, *written*) by human beings, to human beings, in definite contexts, in a language they share: *hence* the obsession with the use of expressions. "The

meaning is the use" calls attention to the fact that what an expression means is a function of what it is used to mean or to say on specific occasions by human beings. That such an obvious fact should assume the importance it does is itself surprising. And to trace the intellectual history of philosophy's concentration on the meaning of particular words and sentences, in isolation from a systematic attention to their concrete uses would be a worthwhile undertaking.... A fitting title for this history would be: Philosophy and the Rejection of the Human.

Cavell arrives at the rediscovery of the ordinary through the elaboration of a skeptical approach to language and to human phenomena. For him, the rules that people devise for talking (what to say and when) are attempts to put oneself in harmony with the other members of the community and with "claims to community." Cavell calls them initiation attempts, borrowing the word from anthropology for initiatory practices that adolescents must complete in order to become part of a community.

In this sense, the ordinariness that Cavell speaks of is not dominated by the preoccupation of knowing whether what I say or mean is also valid for others, but rather by the importance of acknowledgment—that is, recognizing the other and myself face to face with him; recognizing that we are part of the same entity (from the fact that we are both here). It is as if Cavell were introducing an idea of pertinence, which shifts from the idea of contextuality to that of an inevitable involvement in the here and now; a conformity that we have used to attempt to define everyday morality in the early chapters of the present book. "The mental states of one's fellow man are not the object of theoretical interest," Sparti writes, "but the root of our interpersonal ties and our practical commitments—our practical obligations—to others."

Traditional philosophers would say, with a good dose of skepticism, that this is no assurance that the awareness we have of what others mean to say and of what they understand of what we mean is certain. Sparti again: "But it is the very concept of certainty that finds no application in that setting of human relations that Wittgenstein and Cavell call 'forms of life.'"

Cavell addresses the ultimate skeptical question: "And if you wish to know how I know that there are other human beings, the answer is: because I know I have... duties to them. I also know it because I love some of them and hate some of them; but neither loving nor hating discharges me of my duties toward them."

It is from this philosophical background, in a close dialogue with the arguments of Cavell, Austin, and Wittgenstein, that the idea of an "anthropology of ordinary ethics" has arisen. For several years now in field work, in monographs on a specific culture, in collections of articles, in books, and even in university chairs (at first in the United States and then, timidly, in Europe), this new approach has made progress. Not that traditional anthropologists have embraced it, but in some manner it is precisely the "crisis of values," the "fall of ideologies," and a broader interest in religious anthropology that have raised new questions and brought new breakthroughs. Along with this development, another one has emerged from overall changes in the world, to a mixing up of individuals thanks to globalization and the greater mobility, voluntary and involuntary, offered to individuals. The anthropology of ordinary ethics is an attempt to account for new situations of contact and conflict, new individual and collective levels that intersect, and the personal and collective crises and transformations that these produce.

7
Is It Really a Morality?

Three things are indignities for a respectable person:
I have lied, I have farted, I have stolen.
Fulani proverb

The Manyika of Zimbabwe, who are part of the
community that speaks the Shona language, share this
proverb with the Fulani. Anita Jacobson-Widding, who
has studied them for some ten years, confesses that she
finds it difficult to translate the English term "morality" into Shona. She states:

> I tried to find a word that would correspond to the
> English concept of "morality." I explained what I
> meant by asking my informants to describe the norms
> for good behaviour toward other people. The answer
> was unanimous. The word for this was *tsika*. But
> when I asked my bilingual informants to translate
> *tsika* into English, they said that it was "good
> manners." And whenever I asked somebody to define
> *tsika* they would say: "*Tsika* is the proper way to greet
> people," or else "*Tsika* is to show respect." This does
> not merely illustrate the relativity of morality, but

rather the difficulties involved when we try to turn one of our own culture-specific abstractions into a subject of investigation in a society where people do not even have a term for that concept. How can we elaborate methods for the ethnography of moralities in other cultures, when the concept of morality does not exist?

Jacobson-Widding quite rightly observes that the same thing is true of other concepts such as "self," "thought," "emotion," and "society." In order to have a concept of morality comparable to the one that our own society has elaborated, there needs to be a concept of conscience, of guilt, and of responsibility. She offers her own definition of morality: "Morality concerns the norms for good behaviour insofar as this behaviour affects the well-being of any other person than the actor him- or herself."

However, Jacobson-Widding notes, that definition involves an idea of the "other" as an object and of the other as "all other persons"—that is, it implies a separation between the others and myself and the idea of an equality among all subjects. In our own culture, what is more, we distinguish between personal shame regarding the transgression of a norm and guilt, which involves the effects that such behavior has on other persons. When we look at the proverb that the Fulani share with the Manyika, what have we? Is it about shame or guilt? For the Manyika the problem is irrelevant because all three of the actions mentioned—lying, stealing, and farting—imply an inability to retain oneself, a lack of self-control. "Self-control" in this sense is the matrix of respectable behavior.

But in order to understand how this self-control regards some people and not others, we need to consider that all within the community are not considered equal; there are separate categories of inferiority and superiority that have to do with differences of origin or kind. Correctness and good behavior—*tsika*—have to do with knowing how to respect these differences and these hierarchies. Jacobson-Widding explains:

> To know how to show other people respect in the proper way is essential for anyone who wants to be regarded as a "good person." You will show your respect, first, by presenting yourself face-to-face, while avoiding eye contact. Second, you must know how to present a message, a gift, or an expression of gratitude. Third, you must observe the correct bodily posture. But most of all, respect is a matter of greeting. It is by the way you greet another person that you will acknowledge his or her social identity, and your own as well. If you are a man greeting a woman, you should sit on a bench, keep your back straight and your neck stiff, while clapping your own flat hands in a steady rhythm. If you are a woman greeting a man, you must place yourself on the floor, then curb your back and neck, and form your hands into the shape of a round pot, while clapping them quietly. If two women meet, they will not curb their bodies as much as when they meet a man, but when a man meets another man, he will observe an even more stiff, erect posture than when greeting a woman. He will avoid the other man's gaze, and keep his body and speech under strict control.

All of this seems to have more to do with a code of honor than a moral code, but Jacobson-Widding concludes that in some African societies, "social personhood is defined by reference to fixed social categories, which are supposed to be hierarchically related. In these societies, two interacting individuals of different social categories will represent their respective categories more than themselves."

As can be seen from this example, the "ordinary" ethics of the *tsika* corresponds poorly to the idea of morality that has developed in our own society. Rather, it corresponds to a code of behavior, a collection of rules for living well or rules of etiquette—a *galateo*. It might lead to an immediate judgment (or condemnation) of that society for its lack of egalitarian sentiment, for its scarce respect for women, and for the very idea of hierarchy. But although this local "ordinary" ethics does not satisfy us, it nonetheless corresponds to the "moral" rules that a particular human group has given itself. It is as if the need to give common norms were "simply" something that cannot be left out of consideration. It raises the suspicion that we have here a management of "exteriority," of morality as a form of exteriority in which the coherence of appearances is fundamental.

From the rules of a nomad camp to those of an illegal *asientamento* on the outskirts of Buenos Aires, of a tribe in the forest but also of an urban population, the fact of "being together" immediately postulates common norms and is even defined by giving oneself those norms. It is unnecessary for anyone to write them down or pronounce them: these norms are made as the community spreads and following the way it structures itself on a daily basis. There is perhaps no better illustration of this point of view than "Dzhan" in *The Fierce and Beautiful World: Stories* by Andrei Platonov. Even a wounded and dispersed community in a situation of transition faces the constitution and reconstitution of a common rhythm governing "life's events." When Wittgenstein speaks of forms of life, he means forms that are not given from the outside of the human community that produces them; forms of life that not only are forms, but that form life, that gives life the form it needs to unfold.

Anthropology intuits that the normative basis of a society is the society itself and is what keeps it dense and united. That intuition is emptied of every metaphysical idea of society, however. Society gives itself rules because there is a conviviality that precedes every written rule. This is what Joanna Overing and Alan Passes show in the book that they edited on the aesthetics of conviviality. Conviviality is not uniquely a taste for being together; it is also the constant care taken so that such a being together "holds," along with all the ways to make it last (techniques, myths, relationships with the ancestors and with the generations to come, etc.). It is a form of "love and anger," both individual and social. Even if Overing and Passes borrow the term "conviviality" from Ivan Illich, we should keep in mind that the *convivium* is essentially a form of common meal carried on thanks to a taste for and an almost erotic pleasure in being together.

Daily ethics is neither a closed system nor a tradition, however; it is instead a dynamic equilibrium shared among things that are not said or written. This theme quite obviously opens the way for others, among them that of the relationship between these forms of life and others that coexist with them or exist elsewhere. What we are dealing with here is a problem of internal functioning. Clearly, we on the outside "get lost," not only because geographical parameters are lost, but also because we lose ourselves in others' rules. This is exactly why getting accustomed to another culture is a long and difficult task.

8
What Sort of Morality Is This?

Here they are, here are the men who cut off the
  heads,
with their earrings, those who cut off the heads.
  Song of the Ilongot girls

Up to this point we have encountered "everyday
moralities" that may seem to us singular, repugnant,
and far from our own criteria, but what happens if we
arrive at the limit and instead encounter a system of
rules and forms of life that call, for example, for ritual
homicide? How is it possible that a human group
manages to give itself a morality that involved the elim-
ination of other individuals? If we think about it, this is
a bit the warrior morality expressed in the *Iliad*, a
morality that shows signs of a vision of mercy, however,
in a tale that offers both the greatness of the warriors
and pity toward the defeated in the story of Achilles
and Hector.

An anthropologist who died before her time,
Michelle Z. Rosaldo, and her husband, Renato, lived
for various stretches of time with the Ilongot, a proud
and warlike population of hunters and horticulturists in

the Philippines, in the province of Nueva Vizcaya in northern Luzon. After a first session of field work in the late 1960s, Rosaldo and her husband returned to the Philippines in the mid-1970s. On their second visit the anthropologists brought with them the materials they had recorded some years before and they settled down inside the village. Their hut came to be frequented by the inhabitants of the village, who were curious to hear their own voices and their own songs from the past. One evening, the Rosaldos organized a gathering to listen to certain war songs that they had recorded on a special occasion during their first research sojourn. These were songs and chants that praised a value that the Ilongot considered to be fundamental, that of the liget, a youthful rage, a vigor of life at its full, including the desire to kill, to cut off the head of an enemy or even a member of another nearby tribe. On that evening the entire village gathered in and around the anthropologists' hut. When Michelle turned on the recorder a sudden silence descended on the group, and then, while the earlier war songs were playing, slowly, one by one, visibly disturbed Ilongots got up and left the hut. Michelle took this as a personal offense, feeling that she, who had gone to such trouble to have them hear those songs, was being treated with distraction and disdain. Only several days later informants who were close to her explained that what she had given them to listen to had become "insupportable" to the ears of the Ilongots because in the intervening time they had encountered missionaries who had indoctrinated them and persuaded them to abandon their cruel customs and embrace a faith made of messages of love for one's neighbor. The Ilongots had accepted Michelle's invitation, but when they heard the war songs, which reminded them of the perturbing sentiment represented by the *liget*, they were deeply upset. In the system of the *liget*, mourning and rage were closely connected. The desire to kill someone and cut off his head was not only the initiation that young males had to pass through in order to find a female companion and pass into adult life, but was also a response to the death, even the death from malaria, of a member of the village. If someone in the tribe died, the others fell into a rage so strong that it could only be resolved by taking off, singing war songs, in search of someone to kill. This youthful fury underlain by homicidal tendencies was the base, the cement, the very meaning of life in its dangerous plenitude; it represented the nostalgia of the elders for their own lost vigor and the ambition of the young to be recognized. Irascible youths often fought among themselves to prepare for the future ritual homicide, while the young girls sang:

> Here they are, here they are, the men who have cut
> off heads
> with their earrings, those who have cut off heads
> Here we are, here we are lined up, the girls
> with their red tunics, all the girls
> Ah, like grapevines that bend, the flanks of the
> killers and of the girls.

It is not by chance that the book in which Michelle Rosaldo recounts these tales is titled *Knowledge and Passion*, because in the vision of themselves and their own group life, the Ilongot did not distinguish between passion and a vision of reality, between emotions and forms of life. Even having accepted a transformation owing to contact with missionaries, in their deep beings they remained "head-hunters" and suffered from no longer being able to be so.

What kind of morality is this? Is it possible that an entire community was held together by this violent cosmology? Yes, obviously, it is possible, and there are many similar cases. Suzette Heald (*Manhood and Morality: Sex, Violence and Ritual among the Gisu*) reports on an analogous case concerning an African tribe, the Gisu, in which morality is judged on the basis of males' capacity for violence.

It is not by chance that even here a form of morality resides in the interplay between genders, between male and female. For the Gisu, masculinity "must" express itself in the male potential for violence, and specific rituals reflecting that need mark adolescents' passage into adulthood. Heald recounts that even if violence is contained and ritualized, its potential presence creates an interplay between the sexes and forms the tie that keeps the group united. She too wonders how it could be possible that a "machismo" of the sort could be the basis of a morality, but her answer is not far from the one that can be read between the lines in Michelle Rosaldo. There is an emotional division of the field in which the daily life of the tribe is represented that makes it possible for men and women to construct their own identities in an almost angry tension through confrontations with the outside world.

9
A Parenthesis

Still, the question, "What does this have to do with morality?" arises anew, precisely because we are accustomed to an unavoidable barrier, that of "Thou shalt not kill," which, together with a few other commandments ("Thou shalt not bear false witness against thy neighbor," "Thou shalt not steal," and perhaps the commandment against jealousy, the one about not "coveting thy neighbor's goods") filtered down from Judeo-Christian monotheism to the structures of our daily life.

Is it possible that there might be cultures and societies in which it is not evident that eliminating the life of someone is insupportable, elicits scandal and immediately leads to reprobation and disdain? Such cultures not only have existed and still exist, but they are understandable precisely within the notion of "valor," understood as warriors' valor. In a text of Amartya Sen on lay culture in India, there is a repeat of the famous story of the dialogue in the *Mahabharata* between Arjuna, the hero, and Krishna, the divine incarnation, before battle. Arjuna is a "valorous" warrior, but he knows that his brothers are on the other side and that if he fights he must kill them. He is unsure about what to do. Krishna exhorts him to follow his karma and pushes him into battle. Arjuna is a warrior, and for him it is in the act, in the coherence of the act, that what he "should do" finds expression. Amartya Sen says that this is an answer and not an answer because the *Mahabharata* puts both truths on the scales and leaves it up to us to decide. For Sen, the truth of the warrior's valor is a truth of "exteriority"; of a system of coherence within a horizon in which the karma—that which in some manner precedes us—is the *a priori* of our being "in a certain manner" of the world that leads us, as the virtues lead us, and as our own knowledge of how to act leads us. The Ilongot, who suffer as they listen to the songs they sang when they still cut off people's heads, are in some sense led by the virtues connected for generations of the valor of the warrior. On the other hand, however, in Arjuna's "compassion," there is a leap beyond the tribe. Better, there is a relativization of karma, of "destiny," of social and tribal "imprinting," and there is a deep-seated nature, for which in daily life moral cosmologies are not fixed once and for all, but are subject to unexpected developments and to transformations of lived experience. We shall see below what this means and to how great an extent that elasticity differentiates between the moralities of every day and "universal" moralities.

One small observation on the ten commandments: In the way in which they are entrusted to Moses on Mount Sinai, there is something that goes beyond the tribal condition. "Thou shalt not kill" is a bridge launched beyond not killing those who are like yourself; those who belong to your own tribe. But in the list of the ten commandments we still feel the ancient tone of the tribe: there is "Thou shalt not covet thy neighbor's wife," which, in a patriarchal regime, obviously does not provide for the contrary; there is "Honor thy father and thy mother," which has much to do with the basic structures of tradition; there are the structures against committing "impure acts" that envelop sexuality within an idea of contamination and purity that refers back to the distinctions and avoidances of a society that wants to protect itself from unwanted mixtures. Still, in the ten commandments, in later interpretations of them, and in their appropriation by Christianity and, in part, by Islam, there lies the entire substance of the relationship between moral systems that present themselves as universal and those that are instead connected to the quotidian. If today we speak of rights of the individual and human rights (see the later chapter on the topic) it is because some religious "revelations"—the *Mahabharata* among others—have managed to poke their heads outside of the confines of the tribe.

But perhaps the wisest word on the Ten Commandments came from the great Krzysztof Kieślowski with his *The Decalogue* (1989), ten films on the commandments. As a Pole and as a man of faith (but of a very "modern" faith), Kieślowski explains and exemplifies the commandments in ten episodes in which he recounts exceptions to them. It is as if he were saying that one cannot leave daily life out of consideration, nor the extraordinary elasticity that it represents, even in the face of rules that seem immutable. As if from within the horizon of a land as Christian as Poland (at the time) it were possible to tell the truth about a humanization of the commandments that has something to do with the movement against the "repugnance of the human" typical not only of philosophy but also of all theologies.

10
Taboos

1. Do not kill or eat dolphins.
2. Do not raise little goats or eat their meat.
3. Do not point at whales with your finger.
4. Do not sell turtle meat.
5. Do not speak the *merina* dialect in certain specific places on the sea.
6. Do not throw out crab shells in the middle of the night.
7. Do not laugh while you are eating honey.
8. Do not have intimate relations with brothers or sisters of the sex opposed to your own.
9. Do not eat chicken.
10. Do not eat *lovo* [a bearded fish].
11. Do not tame lemurs.
12. Do not wash a dead body after sunset.
13. Do not tear live animals to pieces.
14. Do not pull out facial fair (on the chin, not the eyebrows).
15. Do not eat skate liver.
16. Do not cut down *farafatse* trees to make a canoe.
17. Do not wear red and black clothing.
18. Do not raise pigs and do not eat their meat.
19. Do not attend burials.

> Rita Astuti, "La moralité des conventions: Tabous ancestraux à Madagascar"

Rita Astuti, the anthropologist who reports this list of taboos (*faly*) collected among the Vezo, sea nomads of Madagascar, explains that the first eight are valid for everyone; numbers 9 through 12 apply only to those who have inherited them from their ancestors; those from 13 to 15 apply only to women (the last of these only to pregnant women); number 16 applies only to the husbands of pregnant women; and the last two apply only to those who are possessed by spirits. Astuti has attempted to understand what type of prohibitions these are, and in particular how they are explained by the Vezo. They respond that they really do not know, and that they would willingly do without them if it were not for the ancestors, considered as the source of everything, from whom they have inherited these taboos and who would be offended if they failed to be respected. There are ways and rituals by which an individual can cancel one taboo or another, but these procedures are complicated and at times costly. Still, despite the admitted absurdity of some of them, the Vezo cannot complain because, they say, they have fewer taboos than their neighbors, the Antandroy. The claim, for example, that Antandroy women were prohibited from complaining or crying out during childbirth because the ancestors do not like it. Vezo women in childbirth feel themselves to be much more fortunate than their neighbors because they can howl as much as they like.

The Vezo taboos have no obvious utility in their daily life, nor is it clear why the ancestors established them. And yet they are respected, even if people complain. Aware of the absolutely arbitrary nature of these prohibitions, the Vezo people respond that taboos are what distinguishe human beings from animals. The taboos render humans capable of being moral agents; they make them capable of not doing certain things, capable of limiting themselves and of giving themselves rules. If this were not so, the tribe would have nothing that distinguishes it from a generic cluster of people.

What kind of morality is this? It is not a morality of violence, as with the Ilongot, but rather a morality of arbitrariness, a morality without a motive, a morality of the "caprices" of the ancestors who went before them. Astuti explains: "The *faly* permit the desires and the intentions of the ancestors to give form to the current life of their descendants, whatever the unreasonable, arbitrary, difficult and, by definition outdated nature of their desires."

This may perhaps be the reason for taking on apparently arbitrary prohibitions: the more arbitrary the rules, the more they explain the "gratuitous" means by which a human group gives itself coherence, sets certain norms, and follows certain practices. It is as if the taboos were simply a way to activate a capacity for conforming, for having an everyday morality; as if they were the platform on which the community can then construct its own collective responsibilities and its own group connections. The rules are not important for their content (the *faly* are not considered intrinsically good or bad), but rather for their "propaedeutic" value. In the list, which we read with stupor and amusement, there is a sort of "exercise," a trial, a gymnastic move, an artifice, an experiment of a common "knowing how to do" rooted in a common "do not do." Precisely: a morality of conventions.

11

Cambia, todo cambia

Cambia lo superficial
cambia también lo profundo
cambia el modo de pensar
cambia todo en este mundo.

Mercedes Sosa, "Todo cambia"

The chapters that follow in some ways overturn the impressions offered by the many histories of everyday morality systems. Fractures or total turnovers can break the apparent continuity, without a ripple, of the daily routine of the Vezo people, the Ilongot, or any community. Daily life can explode from one moment to the next when the substratum of rule that structures it cracks. We cannot take it for granted that, on the level of daily life, things will "take care of themselves" forever. In reality, we know that at times things are like banked live coals: we see this in the world today when, as in the Balkans, some groups find local differences of style an excuse for ferocious hatred. Everything seems tranquil, up to the moment that everything explodes. The point is to ask ourselves what is happening when two systems of daily life collide; when, within one system, individual histories and collective rules clash;

when laws and rules of another and more globalizing dimension are inserted into local systems.

Wikipedia informs us that the suffix *-alem*, from the Latin *universalem*, indicates something "that belongs," that "is common to the beings of the homogeneous group referred to." Here is the critical point, or the moment at which groups of a different daily life intertwine. Because daily lives, too, have their "substrata" of rules and cultural codes that are not easily shared. This is hard enough for a traveler, but for anyone who must join substratum unfamiliar to him for a long time or forever there are more serious problems. If there is an everyday morality, it should be able to unfold—perhaps with particular modalities—both within the system that we belong to (our universe) and among differing systems. But how? On the level of everyday life, what are really the moments of articulation among different systems?

The cases that follow are all a part of this difficult and complicated constellation of change. "Cambia, todo cambia," Mercedes Sosa sang many years ago, and some societies are better equipped to accept change than others, and some structures of daily life succeed better than others for us. When one culture collides with another, with the rest of the world, or with a dimension that supercedes the local, the rules that we sometimes call "laws" and "rights" emerge, and, in particular, those rules that claim to be universal and strive to go beyond the single context. It is within the articulation between the everyday morality and a morality that claims to be universal that the future of tolerance lies—tolerance in its dual sense of a tolerance among cultures, but also of the tolerance of a specific culture that prevents it from being crushed by universal claims and does not constrain its members to take as a "superior morality" something that is instead only an "everyday morality."

In the chapters that follow we shall see various cases of transformation, in both a positive and negative sense, of systems of daily morality. Some will recount "success" stories, stories of adaptation and of the capacity for transformation of a given society that manages to "update" its own daily morality in order to respond to changes in both the nearby world and the more remote world. There will also be cases in which this does not happen and the society loses both consistency and its ability to be a daily horizon of reference. There will also be cases of conflict between individual destinies and collective destinies. It is relevant that these case studies include both small groups (tribes, which anthropology once called "simple societies" or "cold societies") and entire cultures, entire countries and nations (which used to be called "complex societies") precisely because an everyday morality can embrace communities of hundreds or millions of people. It is as if there were a "natural" tendency for humanity to cluster around systems of everyday rules that make up the stuff of which it is made and give a sense of reality as something specific in the here and now.

We are aware that the material we are dealing with is resistant, and it obliges us to ride its surf on a number of levels. For this reason, the chapters that follow are under the sign of another song, Brazilian this time: as Marisa Monte sang some years ago, echoing a magnificent *choro di favela*, "Lágrimas, tormentos, quantas desilusões."

12
Lágrimas, tormentos

Lágrimas, tormentos
Quantas desilusões
Foram tantos sofrimentos e decepções
Mas um dia o destino a tudo modificou.
Marisa Monte, "Lágrimas e tormentos"

A. The Case of Nadia

In October 1997, Nadia, a Norwegian girl who was the daughter of Moroccan parents who moved to Norway when they were in their twenties and later gained Norwegian citizenship, was featured on the front page of the newspapers because she had been kidnaped by her parents, who took away her documents and took her to Morocco against her will to marry a Moroccan man whom they had chosen for her.

Nadia, who at the time was eighteen and thus was of age according to Norwegian law, suddenly disappeared from the store where she was employed. It was she herself who called colleagues and let them know what had happened to her. Her colleagues informed the owner of the store, who in turn called the police, who contacted the Ministry of Foreign Affairs.

The Norwegian ambassador in Morocco was charged with negotiating the release of the girl. Negotiations were intense and difficult because of the two countries' different ways of understanding citizenship: as far as Morocco was concerned, Nadia was not yet of age (which she would be at the age of twenty) and was Moroccan, because she was under the tutelage of Moroccan parents (anyone born Moroccan remains so for his or her entire lifetime).

At first the girl's father promised to free the girl. He then retracted his promise, but eventually, after three weeks, he himself paid for her airline ticket to Oslo. Nadia's family enjoyed a subsidy from the state and lived in an apartment paid in good part by public assistance, and Nadia's father was afraid of losing these benefits as a result of the accusations that had been made against him. After her return to Norway, Nadia denied everything that she had said in her telephone calls to her colleagues. She said that she had left for Morocco of her own volition, without any compulsion, because her grandmother, with whom she was close, was ill. Her parents stated that they were preparing a denunciation for defamation against the state authorities and the newspapers and intended to ask for damages. In the meantime, however, the legal case had gone ahead, and a year later Nadia's parents were called to trial for a suit against them by the Norwegian state for "having forcibly held someone against her will." (This is all described by Unni Wikan, here in her article, "Citizenship on Trial: Nadia's Case," in *Daedalus*.)

At this point the Norwegian state requested the aid, as a consultant, of the anthropologist Unni Wikan, a woman well known in Norway for having worked for many years in such Islamic countries as Egypt, Oman, and Indonesia, and who had followed the trial and had occasion to speak with the protagonists. During the trial the parents repeated their affirmation that Nadia had lied, and that she had gone with them spontaneously to visit her grandmother. They admitted that there had been problems with their daughter, but they blamed them on bad company and bad influences (claiming that friends had led her into drinking, smoking, and coming home late at night), and they declared that they had acted purely for the good of their daughter. Wouldn't other Norwegian parents have done the same? They also testified, behind closed doors, that they had taken their daughter to a Moroccan healer to cure her of the bad influence of the jinn, evil spirits. In any event, they were modern parents, integrated into Norwegian society, but who also belonged to an extended Moroccan family.

Nadia made her appearance in court after her parents had completed their deposition, her face covered by a "black blanket" because of the heavy responsibility of having her mother and father brought to trial. Standing up, fragile but very decided, she returned to her original assertions, saying that she had taken them back only out of fear of the consequences for her family. Now, however, another fear seized her even more strongly: that her parents would take her away again and might do something similar to her younger sister.

She spoke of herself as someone who had fought to be what she felt herself to be—a normal Norwegian girl—which was why she had refused a marriage with a young Moroccan that she stated (but could not back up with evidence) had been planned by her parents. She related that several months before these events, she had contacted social services to complain of abuse from her father, who hit her because she used makeup, went dancing, had a boyfriend (a

Pakistani), and worked as a clerk. The social services had offered her protection until she reached eighteen years of age, but then had obliged her to return to her family against her will.

After a number of other witnesses (the grandfather stated, "I thought Norway was a democracy where there was justice before the law" but thought himself mistaken, given that the word of a young girl bore more weight than that of her family), the court, although not recognizing the accusation of forced matrimony, considered the parents guilty of having constrained the girl to act contrary to her own will, gave them a suspended sentence (in an attempt to keep open the possibility of a family reconciliation), and obliged them to pay a fine. Wikan had a role in persuading the court to make the penalty as light as possible, given the significance that prison would have had on the level of the breaking of kinship ties and the reaction on the part of the Moroccan and Islamic community in Norway. However, the case established a precedent in relation to the importance of the crime committed. The verdict was centered on questions of citizenship, thus showing the complexity of the topic. By having decided to request Norwegian citizenship for themselves and their children, the parents had implicitly accepted Norwegian rights and duties, if not on the emotional level, at least on the juridical one. It was unthinkable that Moroccan law be applied to a Norwegian citizen during a visit to the country of origin, as the defense had argued.

Muhammad Bouras, the highest Islamic religious authority in Norway, declared after the sentence that it was "an insult to all Muslims." He added, "The charges and the verdict are an offense against the family and us Muslims. The judge is requiring us to respect Norwegian laws, but he does not show us any respect."

After the trial Nadia went to live on her own, in an undisclosed place in order to protect her from possible retaliation and from the threats expressed by her community. Until today she has maintained an absolute reserve about her case and about herself, refusing to be interviewed or photographed.

Unni Wikan has continued to investigate cases such as this one, and for that reason she has often been accused of being a reactionary who defends the state against the traditional and profound rules of communities, as she states in *Generous Betrayal*, in which she has collected her experiences during the past few years. As an anthropologist, her detractors say, she should stand behind ethnic "differences." She finds instead that "Nadia's case poses a number of basic questions: what are the limits of cultural tolerance? How do we balance respect for human rights with respect for cultural difference?... And how can we enforce the law in the case of violations that were committed with the best of intentions, such as to protect one's child from harm?" Wikan continues:

> Nadia's case has a moral lesson, as I see it: human rights must take precedence over what may be termed, for lack of a better expression, cultural rights. Human rights are based in moral individualism: they are entitlements of the individual as against the state, the family, the church, or other controlling powers. And they apply across the board in liberal democracies. There can be no distinction made on the basis of ethnicity, religion, or other factors. Equality applies, as does the right of exit from the group, as Nadia and Aisha have chosen. The policy implications are these: a plural society requires a social contract to protect the rights of all members. A strong state, not a weak state, is the best guarantee of human rights.

If there is a reflection to be made on the basis of Nadia's case and Wikan's observations, it is that the problem is posed precisely because we cannot give a cultural code or an "ordinary" ethics the value of a "universal" morality. We are faced with two completely different levels. It is one thing to keep to a series of norms that permit conformity and living together in the same place but that are more like criteria of "good manners" or "correct behavior," but it is something completely different to think that those criteria are applicable as a morality above contingencies and beyond their aspect as continually negotiable. Obviously, from the viewpoint of a certain Muslim discourse, ordinary ethics and morality are intertwined, and this is in fact the radical point of dissension with the idea of human rights that the West has developed (and that the Chinese government also sustains every time it is criticized for not respecting human rights). But even in the Islamic field positions are not unanimous, as Mohamed Charfi recalls in his *Islam and Liberty: The Historical Misunderstanding*.

What is a conformity? It is the daily construction of a *cum* that permits living together. In the idea of conformity we already find a negative judgment, as if only the isolated individual were conceivable. But the isolated individual is an abstraction that is highly useful for the sphere of human rights and for that of the law, but it is less useful if we want to really comprehend how persons, settled human groups, communities, and populations act to remain together without massacring each other or scattering. Conformity is the almost dance-like ability to put our own body next to other bodies without bumping into them or actually dancing with them. It is an art of living, the right manner for this precise situation and this specific moment, which tomorrow will both be different. To conform means to be capable of going beyond the rigidity of forms: to "con-form" oneself is not only to form oneself *cum* (together), but also to give form to an aspect that is not exclusively individual. The forms of the quotidian, Wittgenstein's forms of life, are not truly norms and not truly rules: they are norms and rules that have to conform to one another continually, under the threat of seeing society become rigid and culture—everyday culture—transformed into a straightjacket.

It can happen that certain individuals who are part of a culture with strong customs come to realize that if there is a good way to be in the world, it is not to remain mired down by the moral aspect of one's own rules. This consideration already implies a certain detachment. Anyone who is gifted with it also feels that he belongs, but not totally, to the context, to conformity, to the rules of the group of which he is a part. And he experiences his own slight or strong extraneity from the group as a both a liberty and a suffering. What had been an enjoyable feeling of being part of something becomes a realization of the absurdity of the quotidian rules given by the majority (the "silent" majority) as taken for granted. He becomes a character in a play by Pirandello or Ionesco. And *One, No One, and One Hundred Thousand* is the strange and painful friction of not being able to be like all the others, who instead take everyday morality as something immutable; as "true" morality. Problems arise here. The rules that a community gives itself are to be respected as long as the permit individuals and groups to deal with the circumstances in which they find themselves living. People like Nadia are crushed between a cultural code proper to a community and a social situation external to it in which that code makes little sense. Nadia is Norwegian, and in order to be completely Norwegian needs to "lose" the protection of the culture from which she comes. If she does not lose it, she is forced to be closed within a horizon that now corresponds to her only partially.

One existentialist current for which anthropologists are also responsible is what is known as "critical anthropology," which exchanges cultures for moral systems as we understand them in our own society, systems of responsibility and guilt and of rights and duties. This idea of morality, as Jacobson-Widding tells us, has very little to do with the rules on which a human group becomes a compact entity. If this were not so, we would have to accept the notion that someone goes to prison and is punished because he farts in public or points at a whale with his finger.

If we want to free ourselves from these equivocal questions, it is essential that we distinguish between the form of morality elaborated by democracies and legal traditions (in particular human rights) and cultural forms of being together. In order to do so, we need to distinguish the various levels within our own cultures. But things are not so simple. It is true that it is difficult to sustain, for example, in the case of rules regarding cast connected with Hinduism, that they are not almost as binding as a law would be. And very often "conformities" and everyday moralities seem quite binding. This is what Pierre Bourdieu calls "habitus." He puts us on guard concerning the idea that the various "habitus" are just what people do: they are also the matrix of the future and of continuity. Bourdieu states:

> The conditionings associated with a particular class of conditions of existence produce *habitus*, systems of durable, transposable dispositions, structured

structures predisposed to function as structuring structures, that is, as principles which generate and organize practices and representations that can be objectively adapted to their outcomes without presupposing a conscious aiming at ends or an express mastery of the operations necessary in order to attain them. Objectively "regulated" and "regular" without being in any way the product of obedience to rules, they can be collectively orchestrated without being the product of the organizing action of a conductor.

Bourdieu continues:

The *habitus*... ensures the active presence of past experiences which, deposited in each organism in the form of schemes of perception, thought and action, tend to guarantee the "correctness" of practices and their constancy over time more reliably than all formal rules and explicit norms. This system of dispositions—a present past that tends to perpetuate itself into the future by reactivation in similarly structured practices, an internal law through which the law of external necessities, irreducible to immediate constraints, is constantly exerted.

It is probable that in writing these considerations Bourdieu was thinking of the years he spent doing fieldwork in Algeria and of the patriarchal concept of honor that seemed suspended between a strong past and the advent of a different society in which the very concept of honor was no longer practicable. For him, but also for Unni Wikan, who studied the various facets of the society in Cairo and Oman, honor is a complex of behaviors; it is what we want others to think of us; and it is such a strong motivation that it urges men and women to an extremist coherence and society as a whole to the supervision of all individual lives. But it is also true that a concept of honor that for men can correspond to control of their women and, for women, to prestige is so thickly woven that people abstain from accusing others of dishonor for fear that the accusation rebound on themselves. Wikan (in "Shame and Honour: A Contestable Pair," in the journal *Man*) recounts the story of an adulterous woman in Oman whom no one dared to rebuke because her husband was a miser and for her to have a lover was the only way she could provide generous hospitality for friends and relatives.

Honor is the recognition in the image that those around us have of us as a mirror image to which we conform. It is also something much deeper; it is wanting to be as good as others who "have given an example," who have lived in a worthy manner, and who, before us, have been able to live better than we can.

B. The Urapmin Case: Everyone a Sinner

Christmas 1991 was a particularly harsh Christmas for the Urapmin, a small indigenous group of some four hundred persons in a remote locality in inland Papua New Guinea, in the western region of the Sepik river. It had been a *Hevi Krismas*, because as a whole the Urapmin felt that in those days that should have been solemn the cohesion of the community (divided into "a top group... and a bottom group") was gradually and inexorably coming apart. The disputes were so acute that the religious leaders of the two groups felt obliged to give up all attempts to carry on celebrations and rituals in common, as they had done in previous years. Their inability to get beyond the difficulties to celebrate Christmas in proper fashion left many Urapmin full of shame, to the point that some felt the urge to think about celebrating the holiday in other communities. This was something that would have been unthinkable before.

What had happened? During the course of the year a multinational mining company, Kennecott, had initiated prospecting forays on land parcels that belonged to some of the members of the top group. To do the work Kennecott had employed some of them and had paid others with another mining operation in mind. The Urapmin had never had an opportunity to work for such good pay, and the developments had of course annoyed those of the bottom group and who were for the most part excluded. This imbalance in the distribution of benefits had created such jealously and such strong angry feelings between the two groups that they led with increasing frequency to disputes at even the slightest occasion. Things got so bad that the entire community felt itself faced with immanent collapse and was gripped by an unbearable sentiment of moral failure and self-blame. (In the Christian terminology of the Urapmin, *hevi* signifies problems that lead to sin.) Added to all this was another element of future uncertainty, because during the past year not one marriage had been celebrated, which for a group of four hundred persons was a clear sign of crisis.

In an attempt to find a way out of this dramatic situation, the Urapmin charged the Kaunsil, the person within the community elected to resolve internal disputes (among other tasks), with finding a solution. The Kaunsil proposed a plan that followed the traditional method (still in use) for resolving disputes between individuals, exchanging equivalent goods, here transposed to the collective level represented by the two groups in conflict. Each member of one group had to find someone in the other group (whether they had any quarrel with him or not) from whom they could "buy the shame" or "buy the anger" by bringing him something to give in exchange. Once each party to the dispute had received adequate gifts, the dispute could be considered resolved and relations could return to their normal course.

The story of this "heavy Christmas" is recounted by Joel Robbins in a magnificent book about the Urapmin, their ways of dealing with the cultural changes that had invaded their society beginning in the 1960s, and the moral conflicts that those changes brought with them. (Joel Robbins, *Becoming Sinners: Christianity and Moral Torment in a Papua New Guinea Society.*) The traditional cosmology of the Urapmin is in fact divided between the celebrations of the "will" (and the actions that spring from an individual spirit of initiative) as a value, because it is capable of creating new social relations, and a respect for the "law" (which on various levels defines the scope of human liberties), conceived of as an engagement to respect the "legitimate expectations" present in already existent relations. In short, it is a duty to limit individual desires in order to support the solidity of the group and the group's future. With the constant risk—thanks to the complexity of the system—of "slipping" and becoming a "bad person," setting off disputes for failing to share food, for not doing one's share of field work, for not having made a gift, and more. This explains the importance of the role of the "big men," who are considered to have the art of "successfully exercising their wills" in socially productive ways. Because Urapmin social life is created by this constant tension between will and legality. Relations and social groups (in marriages, commercial agreements, villages, hunts, the cultivation of garden plots, sports, and more) are not structured on the basis of a system of prescriptive rules, but must be created by individual acts. For example, the women are the ones who choose the husband they want, and they do so with a "call" that is a specific act of individual will. The men can refuse, but a man who refuses or who is not "called" by a woman remains unmarried. A society of the sort is the object of continual "torments" because there is a constant tension between individual ambitions and the need to keep the group together.

Although they had never encountered missionaries directly (some tribe members were sent to study with missionaries in other villages, in part in an attempt to reestablish a focus within the religious system of the region), in the late 1970s the Urapmin abandoned their traditional religion and adopted Christianity. What convinced them was, in part, the millenarian Christian cosmology, which sees desires as the source of most evils. How could they maintain group cohesion and at the same time "fence in" desires for possession augmented by contact with globalization? The solution they found was to define such desires as being within the sphere of "sins" and themselves as incurable sinners. This was also the way in which the Urapmin spoke about the crises of their *hevi Krismas*, while from an outside viewpoint and for the anthropologist, that crises clearly seemed connected with the difficulties they were experiencing due to the mining operations in their territory. As Robbins puts it, "Read this way, Kennecott becomes a metonym for all the outside forces of change the Urapmin have experienced in the past four decades, and the despondency of the heavy Christmas stands in for the morally demanding Christianity that forms so many of the frameworks in which they lead their lives."

It is in fact the moral dimension that makes

manifest the contradictions between these two logical systems that structure Urapmin life—the traditional system and Christianity. As Robbins explains, "Every time they honor the indigenous system they fail its Christian counterpart as evidence of their propensity to sin." With the adoption of Christianity, they chose to construct themselves as "ethical subjects under a Christian moral system that condemns the will while at the same time they continue to live in a world that demands they create their social life through willful action. This contradiction is, alongside the loss of taboos, another important source of their conception of themselves as sinners."

The cultural changes of the last few decades, including those brought by the arrival of Kennecott, have thus put the Urapmin in a situation full of contradictions, as if "in midstream," and full of changes incompletely realized. It is precisely that indeterminacy that makes imagining the future, a potentially perfect future, something fundamental for the Urapmin, in order to establish order in the heterogeneity of the "cultural materials" that shape their present. "It was this collective project of imagining a future... that Kennecott's windfall upset. And because the process of imagining the future is so important to the Urapmin, when Kennecott upset it the ramifications were widespread."

It should be stated for the record that the Kaunsil's plan for emerging from the crises was a great success: the exchange of goods produced the desired effects, the situation was resolved, and eventually the Urapmin could celebrate the ritual—which was very important to them—of the *Spirit Disko*, in which both women and men danced frenetically in the dark to Christian hymns until, exhausted and possessed by the spirit, they fell down, "freed of sin." The following Christmas was no longer *hevi*, and the Urapmin were able to hope for a future that would find them united, because their torment was how to reconcile their anarchical impulses as individuals with the need to continue to remain together in spite of all.

If, on the one hand, their history shows how everyday morality can be collectively restored when faced with a serious threat for the entire community, on the other hand it shows how a society with a strong cosmology can, when faced by radical transformations, reinterpret itself by adopting another cosmology. It is a painful process, difficult and put into effect slowly, feeling its way, but it says about aboriginal cultures just the opposite of what people think, which is that they are cultures "congealed" into a specific configuration and that exist "outside the world."

C. When Things Go Badly

But things do not always turn out for the best. It can happen that great and epochal changes place individuals and collectivities at a crossroads where they can easily be crushed. Leaving metaphors aside, groups can find themselves caught up in transformations of their internal history and placed before alternatives not of their own choosing, situations that are doubly restraining in which they do not succeed in substituting a new identity for an old one that gave them secure rules, and individuals and collectivities often remain in a void that is also a void of meaning, hence an enormous source of suffering.

Not always have the indigenous populations of New Guinea been skillful at leaving off one cosmology and taking on another. The paradigmatic case is that of the village of Ilahita, an Arapesh community of two thousand inhabitants.

The Arapesh held to a cosmology that greatly emphasized male power—a power whose source was hidden from women and children—and that made use of secrecy to perpetuate itself. As in other tribal cultures in Papua (and elsewhere, as we have seen in the preceding chapters), morality was gender specific—that is, was constituted around distinctions of gender. Differences between men and women were woven into daily life, and village space was divided into two different and opposing domains. The men ritualized their separation and made it a base for a fundamentally warrior ideology made of bravado, initiations stressing courage, and actual violence. Women were kept out of male societies, which were centered in a "men's house" and expressed in initiation rituals in which adolescent males were taken away from their mothers to make men of them. These ritual practices were opposed by female rituals just as rich in detail and just as secret, as documented in a fine book edited by Nancy C. Lutkehaus and Paul Roscoe, *Gender Rituals: Female Initiation in Melanesia.*

For generations, male Arapesh had maintained the "secret" of the origin of their power, a supernatural origin tied to direct contact with a superior being named (as was his ritual sphere) Tambaran. Ritual included an ample display of illusionism by means of stories, music, flutes, trumpets, whistles, gongs, and bullroarers, all of which were considered sacred and secret and were connected with sacrificial feasts involving mechanisms of alliance and redistribution with the neighboring villages.

Following contact with missionaries, and especially after the great transformation of their internal life, when power was no longer obtained with warlike prowess toward other tribes, but with proximity to the power of the whites, in September 1984 the males of the Arapesh tribe decided, in a sort of collective suicide, to confess publicly to the entire village, that is, to the women and children, that everything had been a farce; that there was no secret and no secret power that gave men a special strength. They announced "the death of the father"—understood to be Tambaran—and the shift to a new situation closer to equality, as the missionaries preached. What happened? Donald Tuzin, who lived for a long time with the Arapesh, had visited the village before and after the "outing" of September 1984. On his return he found the village fragmented, its population fallen into a general depression and incapable of reaching a new sense of the collective. Roles had been shattered, and with them the cohesion of the entire group and the motivations that pushed men and women to construct internal and external alliances and seek internal and external resources. When the "unjust" cosmology of Arapesh masculinity collapsed, it brought down the entire village.

Tuzin discovered that this congenital fragility that had led to the death of Arapesh masculinity had already been implicit in Arapesh mythology, which included an enormous female figure in the person of a dangerous bird with a sharp beak, the Cassowary. The Cassowary was supposed to return one day to put the equilibrium between the masculine and feminine spheres in the Arapesh world back into balance. The story of the revenge of the Cassowary has much to say about the dangers of change and the fact that communities are not always capable of adapting to new circumstances. (All told in Donald Tuzin, *The Cassowary's Revenge: The Life and Death of Masculinity in a New Guinea Society*.)

D. A Changing China

Susanne Brandtstädter, an anthropologist and sinologist who worked for many years in China, recounts how the peasants of Shandong and Fujian experienced the shift from Maoism to post-Maoism (in a piece called, "Fakes: Fraud, Value-Anxiety and the Politics of Sincerity," in Karen Sykes' edited volume, *Ethnographies of Moral Reasoning*.)

Mao had constructed an ideology that attributed to the peasant class the ability to "eat bitterness and live a simple life." That talent made the peasants champions of *suzhi*, or quality, authenticity, in the sense that the peasants' mode of living was considered "authentic" and "sincere" in contrast to city-dwellers, impugned as dangerous for their counter-revolutionary tendencies. Peasants were *par excellence* the class that told the truth of history and needed to remain so in order to unmask every reactionary murmur. The moral standard was to counterpose local people tied to the earth against people from the outside who were not tied to the earth. That moral quality was hereditary in the male line and was considered the foundation of a class struggle built on strongly ritual moments such as the *suku*, in which the peasants recounted how harsh life had been before the revolution, and the *piping*, sessions of criticism and self-criticism in which enemies of the class, identified from time to time as persons who resisted the revolution, were made to kneel on broken glass with a placard around their necks and a high hat on their heads. Mao had defined the essence of the moral quality of the peasants. They were heroes and protagonists of the revolution, and they were to remain peasants, attached to their collectivized lands. The model hero was Lei Feng, an altruistic Stakhanovite peasant faithful to the revolution.

The radical change brought by post-Maoism—that of a "socialist market society with Chinese characteristics" or a "socialist capitalism"—completely overturned roles. Today *suzhi* has become a term applied to the quality of commercial products. To understand what it means, go the market of "fakes" in Shanghai in Xiangyang Park, where in an enormous muddy space you can buy brands like Prada, Versace, and Dior, all counterfeited but at times of an enviable quality. The sellers are, for the most part, peasants or ex-peasants. By the standards of *suzhi* these are counterfeiters and dangerous people who are attacking the quality of the products and the new official word of the development of Chinese society and of the model citizen who consumes quality products. It is what combats inauthentic products and a moral quality of the modern, advanced citizen. The hero of this new phase is Wang Hai, who became famous in the 1990s for buying counterfeit products and unmasking their producers, thus earning a reward. Wang Hai became rich and famous, to the point that he was selected, as a model Chinese citizen, to receive President Clinton when he visited China. A few years later, however, Wang Hai himself was denounced for fraud.

In the meantime, the status of the peasants in China had been turned upside down. Now they constitute the backward portion of the country that has not succeeded and is not succeeding in becoming modernized. Today the peasants are identified with corruption connected with the illegal practices of low-level functionaries and the production of shoddy goods. When peasants move to the city, they remain caught between no longer belonging to a locality (today there are three hundred million people in China who no longer live in their place of birth) but still not being accepted as modern city-dwellers. They are the people "who have no education"; they are the source of problems, defined by Mao as the "peasant question," today transformed into the "peasant problem," which is that of not being "able to make money and knowing how to spend it." Moreover, blocked as they are between two impossible identities, the peasants are beginning to rebel and express their discontent, which means they are considered the source of *luan*, or chaos.

So what is happening? Obviously, the peasants of China are in a situation of total transformation, given the fall of Maoist "essentialization" of their identity. Moreover, under Maoism there were many who experienced the moral contradiction between what was traditionally thought to be a "good person" with a relational qualities, who respects others and their sentiments, and being a "good revolutionary," a quality that was often brutal and vengeful, as happened with many peasants who became red guards. That contradiction remains intact today, because the peasants feel themselves again closed within a stereotype defined by the state. The only way out of this situation, Brandtstädter tells us, is to reappropriate "peasantness" as a value, refusing the consumeristic vortex, reestablishing relations of cooperation, and renewing local rituality in the temples and meeting places. This is to some extent what is happening in the provinces that Brandtstädter has studied, where a redefinition of the *suzhi*, of authenticity, and of quality is being put into effect on the basis, this time, of a defense against bureaucratic corruption, a new demand for peasants' rights (as a provocation, many have set up busts of Mao in their houses), and a local solidarity.

We see here an epochal change in which the moral conformity of daily life has been overthrown more than once. The revolutionary "authenticity" of the peasants was congealed by Maoism, which transformed into a political myth a form of life that was then gradually left to fall, leading to cracks and breaks in a congealed identity that had not had time to reconstruct itself within the provisory nature and elasticity of daily life. Today it has proven difficult to survive this mess, and China as a whole is posing questions about its everyday morality. There is the case of a little girl who was run over by a car while a public camera filmed the scene. No one came to her aid, and the car then backed up and ran her over again (the driver was afraid that if the child had remained alive he would have had to pay an exorbitant indemnity). Public opinion throughout China was outraged. The debate soon transferred to the social networks, where such questions were raised as: What kind of a country have we become if things of this sort take place? What has happened to compassion, mercy, and morality in this new China of individual development and enrichment?

13
Other Torments
(More Familiar This Time)

Less than fifteen years ago a specter invaded all of Europe before spreading all over the world. Its appearance prompted protests and new forms of indignation. It was cited as a clear manifestation of a barbarian trend in customs, and also a worrisome signal of a transformation in the collective psychology. Famous sociologists, linguists, political commentators, and students of customs and daily morality pointed to the cell phone as a clear sign of the decadence of the age. French railways prohibited its use except in special compartments or in glass boxes constructed for the purpose. The Italian railways announced that the use of such an instrument could harm persons nearby. Young people appeared to be the privileged victims of this new instrument's attack on the rules of civil communal living, while adults were divided between some who scornfully promised that they would never use it and those who used it reluctantly, but only for urgent calls and to reassure the wife and children or the husband left waiting at home.

Because of its terrible and sudden spread, the cell phone terrified many who saw in it a clear attack on "discretion." It was unacceptable that one should have to hear the details of others' lives, and in particular had to hear them as if they concerned the unintended listener. Some new cell phone users covered their mouths and the phone with one hand, whispering into it as if they were hiding it in shame from the gaze of others. Caught using one by a railroad conductor, many were fined or simply reproached in public for lack of respect of the rules of civility. What people found particularly worrisome was the spread of its use, left to the preoccupying anarchy of a total lack of rules. It bothered people that someone might speak alone like a madman, walking along the street and gesticulating in the void, and that even respectable (or less respectable) people should answer a cell phone ring while they were occupied in public gatherings such as a party conference, a cultural meeting, or an academic lecture. The more ironic critics made fun of it, inventing jokes highlighting the stupidity of the object, hence the stupidity of the person using it, unconscious of how paradoxical this was.

Decades—or rather only a few years—have passed, and the cell phone has been absorbed, not because we have gotten used to it, but because habit has devised rules for it. Was it so difficult to understand that it could be turned off when it was not needed? Was it so difficult to find a way to eliminate its ring to avoid disturbing people? And then, why should speaking on the telephone with someone not present bother someone who was present? Was waking to someone in a train compartment so bothersome to a third party? How could anyone condemn the normal gossip that people used to exchange in person, face to face, and were now exchanging by cell phone? In this fashion, even the French railroads caught up to the times and understood that yes, in the final analysis, they had exaggerated a bit. The constancy and the widespread use of the cell phone had created rules, criteria, and a minimum common denominator for a new code of polite speech. Still, the disturbance brought by this technological innovation—as had often happened in other cases, as with the train and its new speed: Gandhi was persuaded that the train would destroy the morality of Indian villages—was justified. The mobile phone cut into the division between public and private and between inside and outdoors. It changed the way in which we interpret sounds, our habit of being constantly attentive to grasping different sounds, and even our relationship with our own voice in a public setting and with our tone of voice. As had happened before with great technological innovations, people constructed new behaviors, new situations of ownership and ease, and new avoidances around its use.

The case of the cell phone shows how daily life swallows up innovation, models it and shapes it to its own convenience, and how people manage to devise unwritten rules without even realizing that they are doing so. To be sure, driving a car while writing a text message is dangerous, but only because the producers of cell phones have not caught up with daily life. What is certain is that no one is surprised any more if the ticket seller behind the window in the train station gives a quick look at his incoming text messages while you search for change. It is possible to think that the cell phone or the iPhone has increased our solitude, but it would be a good idea to reread Elias Canetti's observations on how alone and anxious humanity would feel without the telephone. (Elias Canetti, *The Secret Heart of the Clock: Notes, Aphorisms, Fragments, 1873-1985.*) The portable telephone has freed us from the slavery of having to go home to receive telephone calls and has made it possible for us to go back to being "fresh-air people"; it has given emigrants a virtual house where they can be reached by distant friends and given people late to an appointment a way to notify the person waiting for them. It has been a silent revolution in customs, one without too much drama, if we exclude the torments of the sociologists, who are persuaded that only spoiled sons and daughters of well-off families can make use of it and are blind to the fact that they have before them a transformation on a world-wide level in which even the simplest rickshaw driver in Calcutta or fisherman in Kerala uses a cell phone to maintain his survival network.

It remains to be seen what this transformation in customs signifies for the relationship between the interior and the exterior dimensions of daily life. If the telephone has liberated us from having to go home, it has done so in a highly paradoxical manner, putting our house in our pocket, together with the office and the family. To be sure, we are well aware that the cell phone can be turned off, but why should we do so? Once the telephone remained attached to its wall when we left the house; now it comes with us, and turning it off makes little sense. The innovation of the cell phone resides in having modified the consistency and the multiplicity of spheres that make up our daily experience, often reducing them to one (we are—also—our cell phone: we need only think of everything that it contains or does), and fooling ourselves with its "infra-structuring" power. As long as there is good reception and the battery doesn't die.

14

A Question of Scale: Still the Local Mind?

> The private moment and the public one are not adja-
> cent, like a bedroom and a medical clinic, but are
> interwoven. Where the most private event takes
> place publicly, even public things are decided
> privately, thus comport a physical and political
> responsibility, which is something completely differ-
> ent from a metaphorical and moral one. The private
> person takes his own responsibility for public acts
> because he is always in place.
>
> Walter Benjamin, *Kritiken und Rezensionen*

The problem with human rights is that they are thought
of historically as an alternative to the law. They are the
product of the only civilization—our own—that has
expressed, practiced, and constructed a global vision of
the world (and, as a consequence, has elaborated the
notion of universal citizenship). No other great civilization has taken a similar idea into its head, not even
China in its golden ages. From the French Revolution
on, the idea of the "universal" (that is, of a geographi-
cally well situated particular) has been superimposed
ideologically on the world, without ever raising the
problem of understanding whether and how it is possible to articulate the "particular" and the "universal."
There is nothing natural in the idea of a universal citizenship; rather, the condition *sine qua non* for the existence of something of the sort is to remove the idea that
what we call "local mind" could exist. Something gets

left out in this sudden rise in scale, and that something is and cannot be other than the relationship with context. It is the "weft" of cross-references inherent in the process of the construction of meaning—as a conversation among forms, agents, presences, habitudes, tendencies—that is living in a world. That irreducible being "in place" that Benjamin speaks of, which is, however, something else than inhabiting the world. It is a question of scale. If it is true that originally *ethos* (ηθος) signified "the place to live" and from that meaning it then passed to that of "consuetude" (habit or practice), then what we want to speak of comes from there, keeping in mind that a consuetude is a mood and forms a mood—that is, a temperament or character.

In this sense it is perhaps true that what we are doing with the present book is writing, twenty years after *Mente locale* (by Franco La Cecla), a demonstration of the need to reflect today about how the globe can be designated, not letting ourselves be too surprised if, when we travel around the world, we find standing in front of us what we thought we had left behind us (as Franco Farinelli reminds us in his *Il globo, la mappa, il mondo*). For the moment we lack the proper passageways (if these exist) that might permit us to articulate in meaningful terms and collectively (not individually) "local mind" and "general mind," given that the latter cannot be thought of only as a declination of the former.

The impression is that the impossibility of moving from one level to the other, from the particular and the ordinariness of everyday life to morality as something more conscious and more general, and eventually to the idea of a minimal universal morality for everyone, is an impossibility that safeguards the levels of mutual autonomy of the quotidian and the "permanent." Elasticity, the not directly moral quality of having to behave in conformity with the life of others, the mimetic nature of daily life—all this cannot move to the more abstract and decontextualized level of the relation between contexts. There should be some sort of rule among contexts, and perhaps it is what we are accustomed to calling a system of laws that regulate a country. After that we pass on to a "transnational" system, and there particular causes should not come into play or else we run the risk, outlined by Unni Wikan, of a communitarianism that does not respect the rights of the individual person.

What is intriguing is to understand what is involved that impedes communication on these levels. There is a lack of equivalence; the levels are of a different sort, untranslatable from the one to the other. The cushion that keeps them apart is also a transformer that alters the nature of questions as they pass from one level to the other. It is as if their "times" were different. The time of the local mind is embodied in space and is transformed with it (it is a geography, not yet law; it is not *nomos*). The time of the law is an immobilized time, fixed like a butterfly on a pin in a collection box in a shop window; the time of human rights is an out-of-time, something like the temporality of jet lag.

Augustin Berque, a geographer and an orientalist, has pinpointed the problem of the articulation between the differing scales that always confront us:

> Individual subjectivity (*subjectité*) is in continuity with social subjectivity (what is called the collective unconscious or collective subjectivity), but it is not ontologically identical to it because its place is not of the same scale. Social subjectivity is in continuity with human nature, but it is not ontologically iden-

tical with it because its place is not of the same scale. Finally, human nature is in continuity with nature itself (life, matter, universe), but it is not of the same scale. Each on its own scale, these different places of being—the individual, society, humanity, the biosphere, the planet, the solar system, the galaxy, the universe—are soaked in subjectivity. That subjectivity is evident at the scale of the individual place of being, that of the consciousness of "I think"; it is less and less so (because less and less accessible to the consciousness of the individual subject) as the scale of that place rises, but is no less manifest, although in terms that cannot be reduced to those of the scale of being of consciousness.... It is essential, from an ethical perspective, to take into consideration that structure of scale of place of subjectivity. In fact, in this case, confounding the levels leads inevitably to moral irresponsibility and acts contrary to ethics.

The Culture of Ethics offers a reading different from *Mente locale.* In the latter the discovery was the supremacy of dwelling and its obstinate presence despite all attempts on the part of institutions, administrations, and architects to expropriate it. Dwelling, in fact, is not a morality; it is a human faculty, a capacity transmitted and acquired for using space to give a sense of oneself and to take from space a sense of one's own "being there." The local mind represented and still represents a constant dialogue between places and persons in a form of mutual modeling. Here it is clear that morality does not enter into the picture, but that the local mind quite decidedly is a matrix of an agreement to stay together somewhere. To return to Walter Benjamin, it is that always being "in place," that dwelling, that way of being in a place that comports a concrete physical responsibility; that "proximity" that should induce us to recognize, above all, who is our "neighbor."

Writing *Mente locale* was a way of freeing ourselves from the enforced influence of other approaches (sociological, anthropological), beginning with the impression that in discourse about "habitus" or "forms of life" or in talk about social norms or culture following Durkheim there was an incompleteness due to the absence of the "meat" of the world, of the dialogue between the bodies of the world and human bodies in the world. Space and dwelling give back concreteness to a discourse in which otherwise categories remain suspended in a void and give context a tangible dimension, not simply a textual one. The intuition at the time was that in the disciplines involved in "being in the world" there was the same negative imprinting of the "rejection of the human" that Cavell speaks of. Anthropology itself was still crushed within a dimension that was completely textual and of *doxa*, of a classification of the real, and only recently and for disciplinary reasons has it seriously taken on the flesh of the world it had to do with.

Today the point is to understand how to rethink what, as a Western civilization, we have thought for several millennia, which is now vacillating on several levels under the effect of the "global," given that—for some things at any rate—"a place to live in" is in fact the entire world. What are we to do? How can we elaborate a somewhat different way of looking at things?

This is the difficulty, for example, that an environmental ethics encounters when it enters into dialogue with the quotidian. There must be preoccupations for the entire world, but between the level of daily life and that involved in environmental ethics there is a jump in scale. The Baka pygmies of Cameroon know this by personal experience. The international environmental organizations have won the battle for the protection of the rain forest, but the pygmies have lost that battle because they were kept from hunting, that is, kept from using the place in which they live and about which they have the most profound knowledge. In the great environmental battles it is often precisely the indigenous dimension that is not taken into consideration. On the other hand, organizations like Greenpeace have a definite effect on people's daily life because, using the logic of clever campaigning, they have succeeded in combining the quotidian with emergencies ranging from canned tuna to nuclear power stations and from paper for books to refrigerators without HFCs. The question is how to pass from a militant logic to a "normal" logic, to taking care of the place in which we live as part of ordinary behavior. To do so successfully we need to take into account the difference of level that exists between "here" and "the world" and not take it for granted that globalization has liberated us from the need to practice the quotidian. This is not easy, however, and there is something profoundly equivocal in the confusion of levels that still exists between the moral and supranational "big issues" and ordinary ethics. This confusion weighs on other questions such as those involved in human rights.

15
Rights: Human?

> The meaning of the word "nation" thus changed from designating a prepolitical entity to something that is supposed to play a constitutive role in defining the political identity of the citizen within a democratic polity.... The nation of citizens does not derive its identity from some common ethnic or cultural properties, but rather from the *praxis* of citizens who actively exercise their civil rights.
>
> Jürgen Habermas,
> "Citizenship and National Identity:
> Some Reflections on the Future of Europe"

Buddhism came into China from India, introducing universal concepts, the idea of universal constants, and many other abstract notions. Religions and the great classical philosophies seem to fly above the quotidian. But is this really the case? And what if at base what they do is instead the contrary—that is, if they attempt to inscribe the quotidian in a universal dimension? And does not "do not do unto others what you would not have done to you" have both a very concrete dimension and a more abstract one? Are not the *puja* in the Indian world, for example, a quotidian form of that articulation? Even with a cell phone in the breast pocket of the *kurta*?

Like the universal, which claims to enter into daily practice and provide it with a model, but to do so it must pass through the filter of the quotidian and change completely. Like Buddha, who, the more he moves east the more he becomes a woman, the woman who protects: Tara, Canon. Buddha who takes on almond-shaped eyes and hanging ears in China after having passed through the face of the *kouros*, the handsome, curly-haired Greeks of Magna Grecia in Gandhara (now Kandahar).

Religions are born locally and become big thanks to how and to what extent they prove able to develop and adapt after successive sedimentations, being broken up, or torn apart. Revelations are a form of "local minds"—the tables of the law are Sinai, the surahs are Mecca or Medina; the illumination is the Bo tree of Bodh Gayā—that succeed in becoming synthesized in a way that allows them to reappear elsewhere. Only once completely unfolded does the virtue of humanity touch the universal, Meng-tzu taught.

Human rights are the lay and modern version of the attempt made by religions of a universal character to be superior to local contexts but retain an influence over them. For example, Buddhism teaches the emperor Aśoka that there is something superior to the pride of war and conquest. In the sculpted rock face near Junagadh, in Gujarat, there is an impressive reference to the quotidian, to the quality of the roads, to the shade that a *pipal* tree must project over the village to permit its social life, and to the idea of a non-violence that becomes the active matrix of collective existence. There are in Christianity and in Islam infinite cases of "bargaining" between universal rules and daily events. Traditional Islam can be transformed, from one country to another, by preexistences; mix with the local cults; take on the *djinn*, the spirits; and adopt the idea of saintliness as heroism or as singularity. This is what Clifford Geertz tells us in his classic work on the differences between Islam in Indonesia and in Morocco,

Islam Observed. Christianity has played a similar role in the relationship with the cult of images, even with what might be considered "idolatry" in the Nahuatl and Aztec cults. One might even read the Catholic institution of the sacrament of confession as an attempt to mediate between the idea of universal morality and the need to accept the infinite exceptions of local contexts and of individual histories. When things go well. Because religions are also the source of a rejection/refusal of the human that leads to conflicts, repressions, the negation of the context, and at times to its total abolition.

      The problem of human rights then becomes not so much to establish what human rights are, but rather to understand what we mean by "human." In this sense, religions have developed an anthropology that human rights lacked, starting by taking context—a context—seriously, and from there enlarging its confines. It is the vagueness and the disembodiment of the human in "human rights" that renders some of the preoccupations of daily life difficult. This is the old problem that the Enlightenment was already posing. What effect does the pain of a mandarin in distant China have on me, and what would I do if I could arrange for his death at a distance, becoming very rich in the process? How much would I feel truly "involved" in responsibility for his unhappiness or for his death? Things have changed since the Enlightenment: the world is now much more connected and "contiguous," but in preoccupation about the future of populations stricken by a flood in southern Madagascar or in Russia there is a somewhat excessive pretense of being truly everyone's "neighbor." I can be so morally, to be sure, but not with the emotions and the responsible involvement of a face-to-face situation. The physical presence of others around me asks something different of me than when someone sends me a petition in favor of the rights of people who are far or very far from me. These are different levels, and mixing them risks preventing the local level from developing and the universal level from having any effect.

Human rights stand halfway between an awareness of the need for rules superior to the local and communitarian context of the local mind and the need to be included in the same particular contexts. They are suspended between "that which is" and "that which should be," a classic suspension of moral philosophy, which has distinguished a level of custom and what people normally do and another level of what they should do, become, or be.

What distinguishes the various sorts of universalism from what people normally do is, precisely, the "natural" and practical efficacy of local rules as against the difficult interjections of abstract and universal rules. Imagining a universal morality implies knowing that we are dealing with the "absolute" desire to do good. And this is the essence of human rights: how to make them understood as something that is truly a part of ourselves and of our daily life, something that we are induced to respect without even having to think about it. We know that things are not like this; that it is difficult to make human rights respected, because they presuppose the idea of a human community of which "everyone foreign to us" is a part, an idea that is not easy to grasp precisely because—Simmel and Kafka had a deep understanding of this, each in his own way—it is a question of a form of precipitation, a hasty rush of distances that brings closer to us something that nonetheless remains distant.

Richard Wilson tells us that human rights emerged at a precise moment in recent history. When the dictatorial regimes in Latin America or the state dictatorships in Eastern Europe began to collapse, some realized that the formula connecting citizenship to an idea of nation, territory, blood, and belonging could no longer and should no longer function. Too many populisms and too many fanaticisms had been based on that idea. What was needed was to construct new democracies on a less contextual and ethnic idea of citizenship. It was then that the question of human rights truly gained in substance. Such rights should represent the lowest common denominator of belonging to one and the same country, without having that belonging work in favor of the country or against it. It is considered fundamental that the subject of rights of a given country be stripped of all contextual connotations of language, religion, race, ethnic identity, ideological adhesion, and conformity to a local or national morality. Human rights strip away the flesh of the subject, but that reduction is essential in order to protect him from specific definitions that risk privileging or marginalizing him. The application of human rights alone left a void between the general level and the local context.

The exemplary case here is that of South Africa, which is emerging from the experience of apartheid and where "culture," defined as differences between the culture of the whites (Afrikaners or whites of other origins) and the culture of the tribes that made up the nation, was put forward as the basis of the constitution. This ideological "culturalism" was, as Adam Kuper, a South African, recounts, what was left of an ideology of land and blood of nineteenth-century origin. The "territories" in which the tribes were enclosed were justified by the idea that for a peaceful life in common it was indispensable to express diversity in terms of spatial separation. Obviously, this justified racism, economic disparity and disparity in access to resources, and a rigorous protection against contacts between the various member groups. When apartheid collapsed, the first problem was how to keep the country united on a basis that had nothing to do with the ideology of diversity. Human rights made an appearance, but above all thanks to the establishment of the Truth and Reconciliation Commission. That commission had the task of judging crimes committed during apartheid. The guilty were guaranteed a degree of clemency if they confessed their own misdeeds to the Commission in public session. This seemed the only way to avoid an endless series of vendettas and retaliations. Between 1995 and 1999, the Truth and Reconciliation Commission set up thousands of public hearings to which the guilty and the relatives of the victims or the victims themselves were called, either to confess or to testify. The idea was that the victims could request a monetary compensation for the terrible harm they had suffered. When all was said and done there were twenty-two thousand victims and the proceedings for compensation became increasingly difficult and complicated. South Africa experienced human rights in a singular garb as the basis for a new social justice and a new country. The entire procedure left many victims and relatives of victims profoundly frustrated and dissatisfied. A good many of them would have much preferred the idea of a visible and much more concrete punishment that was much closer to an idea of retaliation and vendetta. According to Wilson, this is where two differing conceptions of justice clashed, one much more contextual and local and another that is claimed to be above all individuals and all things.

A similar case is that of the Gacaca courts in Rwanda today. Facing the enormity of the massacre—

from eight hundred thousand to a million persons, most of them Tutsi, a true and proper genocide carried out house by house—the government, the Rwandan Patriotic Front, created to render justice and to pacify the population, found itself faced with prisons overflowing with inmates, with over a hundred thousand prisoners accused of crimes against humanity, genocide, and war crimes, and with the perspective of trials that would take over a hundred years to process. At that point, the government reactivated the popular court that had existed in Rwandan tradition, called *gaçaça* and managed by the elders and by persons that the village held to be wise and above the parties. Rwanda has abolished the death penalty and offered, in these courts, the possibility for the guilty to face the victims' kin directly, and to hear testimony pro and con from the other inhabitants of the villages. These Gacaca operate on three levels culminating in a genuine court of appeals, and they have the right to commute sentences of detention, even imprisonment, but also to impose indemnifications and works to the benefit of the village.

The result has been impressive from the viewpoint of admissions of guilt, but also for a reconstruction of facts and the truth. Some ten thousand cases have been brought to trial and concluded, and the effect of pacification on the country has been amazing. Still, on the level of the European Court of Human Rights there is today serious criticism of the excessively artisanal nature of this justice and of the little protection that it offers to witnesses and relatives of the victims against possible retaliation on the part of the condemned's kin.

The Gacaca are nonetheless an example that shows how human rights, in order to be exercised, must find a base in the local sense of justice in a given territory; a justice that adheres more to contexts than to what the abstractions of international jurisprudence can offer.

In an article on democracy in the island of Mauritius, Thomas Hylland Eriksen states that human rights—that is, a minimum common base that connects persons who live in the same place and that can be defined as sharing those same rights (an identity founded on the idea of the rights of citizenship)—is achievable and could easily be put into place in countries like Mauritius precisely because, despite the "patchwork" of its constituents (who are Hindu, Muslim, and descendants of English and French colonisers), they have a highly developed sense of the individual. Now and then, when there is a conflict between individual rights and rights arising from membership in a certain community, it is the latter that give way. Also, during electoral campaigns, which often represent the various ethnic components of the country, what is emphasized is individual rights and a common sense of belonging to the same country.

From the anthropological point of view, human rights are the consequence of a method for understanding human complexity. It was the anthropologists who insisted on the importance of a vision that takes cultural relativism into account. It should be kept in mind, as Marshall Sahlins states, that we are talking about a method for knowing, not a parameter of judgment in which "anything goes," and there is no difference between the idea that it is just to kill an enemy, perform an excision, carry out infanticide, or let clandestine immigrants drown, and the contrary of all these. Sahlins states:

> Cultural relativism is first and last an interpretive anthropological—that is to say methodological—procedure. It is not the moral argument that any culture or custom is as good as any other, if not better. Relativism is the simple prescription that, in order to be intelligible, other peoples' practices and ideals must be placed in their own historical context, understood as positional values in the field of their cultural relationship, rather than appreciated by categorical and moral judgments of our making. Relativity is the provisional suspension of one's own judgments in order to situate the practices at issue in the historical and cultural order that made them possible. It is in no other way a matter of advocacy.

Human rights treat every man as if he were a foreigner. In this sense, it is within the relations between different contexts, between different local minds, that the need arises for that the need arises for a "threshold" (Piero Zanini, *Significati del confine*), for a frontier that defines the rights of the foreigner and the rights of individual to be a "foreigner" to his own community—that is, to excuse himself, if he wants to, from the norms of daily life, on the condition that his withdrawal does not lead to the destruction of other people's daily lives. The relationship between an everyday morality and an exceptional morality is as if suspended. The respect for the context in which one finds himself stands opposed to the respect that any context must have for the individuality of those who are a part of it, "as if that individuality were that of a foreigner." Human rights are, in this sense, based on the older rights of the host and his obligations toward the stranger.

In the case of the Moroccan girl recounted by Unni Wikan, what happens is that Nadia feels herself estranged from the cultural context in which she grew up and is able to choose not to follow it (is this a choice or a different way of expressing her belonging to it?). The idea of a universalism based on the simultaneous existence of different contexts that mediate with one another is, on the other hand, impossible in practical terms. It is only by accepting a position out of context represented by extraneousness that human rights can be defined. In this sense, a nation constructed on a lowest common denominator of human rights is a nation of strangers, and this is one of the most critical aspects of the question (a question that politically correct discourse, for example, has often been unable to or wanted to confront).

The question is whether it is possible to construct a civil cohabitation as George Orwell and E. P. Thompson dreamed of it, based on common decency and which includes egalitarianism, social justice, and environmental justice. This is a "communitarian" idea, in which the community is constituted, for example, by the eighteenth-century working class in England. The conditions that enabled that class and that common decency to be concrete no longer exist. At the time there was a dialectics of force: the moral economy according to which the popular classes demanded the right to subsistence (hence local control of resources: grain, water, woods) was respected by the paternalism of the feudal lords and the nobility. The attempts of the shopkeepers and the financial operators of the time to cut the link between resources and their context was fought by a moral economy for which the life of the popular classes assured the permanence of the classes in power. Today proposing a moral economy would presuppose being able to set conditions for banking, on finance, and global commerce that completely alienate resources from the context for which they would be destined. Derivatives, monetary speculation, and the mobility of the labor force have made it very difficult for any "local mind" to find expression and make itself respected. This does not mean that it a new project of moral economy is impossible, but only that it be thought of uniquely as a move of resistance. Moral economy, as E. P. Thompson has taught, is a dialectics of forces, and in order to be real must reach beyond the utopianism of ideologies and confront the complexity of the real world today. And, as was the case in eighteenth-century England, it is in anger, in protest, and in a capacity for collective expression that the possibility lies that such a dialectic not be extinguished.

It is thinkable that the processes of globalization need a law, along with some indisputable parameters to preserve human communities from all attempts to sell off local resources and manpower. This would imply a complete reexamination of the role that money plays today. Having made money an abstract fetish capable, by its nature, of destroying all human relations and all collective cohesion, has rendered us nearsighted about the thousands of situations in which money is instead used to solidify those relations and to give preeminence to the social tie. This is what David Graeber invites us to do in his book, *Debt: The First 5,000 Years*. Debt is not only the absurd burden that capitalism places on each one of us but is also, originally and in daily life, the way in which people decide to tie themselves to one another by means of money; to have an "obligation" to others. It is a step forward, Graeber tells us, from "an eye for an eye and a tooth for a tooth," precisely because an egalitarian justice based on revenge is not economical from the point of view of the construction of a society.

Anthropologists such as Jonathan Parry and Maurice Bloch had already taught this in their *Money and the Morality of Exchange*, precisely to demonstrate that money itself can be channeled and used to reinforce the ties that keep a human group together, and that it is transformed by the meaning of exchange that people give to money when it is lent, given, or exchanged for a pawn and represents a social good rather than an abstract good.

16

Ordinary Ethics and Aesthetics

Now I am going to use the term Ethics in a slightly wider sense, in a sense in fact which includes what I believe to be the most essential part of what generally is called Aesthetics.

Ludwig Wittgenstein, "Ethics, Life and Faith"

Wittgenstein goes on to say:

My whole tendency and I believe the tendency of all men who ever tried to write or talk Ethics or Religion was to run against the boundaries of language. This running against the walls of our cage is perfectly, absolutely hopeless. Ethics, so far as it springs from the desire to say something about the ultimate meaning of life, the absolute good, the absolute valuable, can be no science. What it says does not add to our knowledge in any sense. But it is a document of a tendency in the human mind which I personally cannot help respecting deeply and I would not for my life ridicule it.

This happens to anyone who travels. There are countries in which the quotidian takes on a particularly noticeably "formal" character in which it seems that the duty of daily conformity has spread everywhere as the right appearance, even the fine appearance. It is as if, in order to be a part of a society, one has to learn to respect a formal elegance taken to the extreme; an elegance that has something to do with doing good and fleeing evil, in the sense of recognizing the right tone, the right color, the right geometries, and the right sound volumes.

Entering a Tokyo restaurant not far from the temple in which the *kamikaze* pilots are remembered, the visitor is impressed by the essential nature of the wood and the absolutely stripped down look of the place. Everything superfluous has been removed. The room that contains the restaurant has nothing on its walls; the wooden plank from which you eat has no ornament and is not even polished. What you eat—raw fish—is exquisite and stripped to its essence, and it is expensive, not because this is a luxury restaurant but is one of the places in which you eat well and the dishes are traditional. There is no recall of any "modernist" style and no concession to what we call "design" (but in reality here everything is "design" in the sense that it is absolutely correctly designed). The place is simply exactly what it should be.

Later, as you walk through the part of the city not far from the booksellers and printers, you come across a pastry shop. In the window there is one small, round pastry, and next to it one long-stemmed flower. There is no *coqueterie à la japonaise* about it: it is simply a pastry shop and nothing else.

That reduction to what is essential continues for the entire voyage, not only in the places you visit, but in behavior, in the expression of emotions, and in saying nothing in preference to speaking. It is as if an entire civilization had a horror of padding. Later you find yourself one evening in Kyoto at a boring official reception at a Western embassy. There is a brief entertainment featuring two very young apprentice geishas. They present a dance of graceful and geometric movements to the accompaniment of a *shamisen* played by an older geisha. At the end of the presentation one of the young geishas shows that she is amused by your curiosity about her headdress, the lipstick that covers only her lower lip, and the white makeup that covers her face and neck and ends in a swallowtail. She looks at you; she sends you subtle sidelong glances and follows you imperceptibly with her interrogative and mischievous air, and you don't know what to say, since your common language is only a few words of English. But the elegance of her gestures, the allusive nature of the way in which the magnificent silk of the flowered kimono moves, and the light steps of her feet in her white *getas* envelop you. You find yourself confused, ensnared, and it seems to you that all of this is only for you, and you are irresistibly led to ask her for an appointment. Up to the moment that she leaves, carried away, and from behind the window of a large black car she turns around to look at you. You return to your hotel disturbed, and after you return to your native land you find yourself holding a book, *The Structure of "Iki,"* in which you find the story of what happened to you in Kyoto. But here it is recounted in exemplary fashion in the 1930s by a Japanese philosopher, Kuki Shūzō, who sought to explain that is the aesthetics of daily life, that elegant nonchalance, that world of appearances that are known to be fleeting, that attitude of haughty disdain that Italians call *sprezzatura* and Kuki Shūzō calls *iki* that communicates that no explanations are needed, except possibly in the way in which a geisha treats you, in her way of looking at you out of the corner of her eye, in her attitude of wrapping herself up in the unsaid.

And then, more calmly, you run into the *Tale of the Shining Prince* (*Genji Monogatari*), a work written in the eleventh century and recounted in magisterial fashion by the historian Ivan Morris in *The World of the Shining Prince: Court Life in Ancient Japan*, where there is an entire world, that of the Heian court in tenth-century Japan, founded on criteria of style and beauty. Morris describes the little-known Heian civilization on the basis of evidence left by a few writers and highly sensitive ladies of the court such as Sei Shōnagon and above all Murasaki Shikibu, the lady author of the *Tale of Genji*, the "Shining Prince," the emperor's son. The center of an aristocratic culture of extreme refinement, the Heian court was founded on a complex social stratification (to the point of including a special rank for ghosts and phantasms and another one for the emperor's cat), in which the aesthetic dimension—in such things as the quality of calligraphy or details of comportment—played a key role in distinguishing between the various ranks. Despite the many intrigues and ferocious power struggles characteristic of this epoch, an interest in and attention to the elegance of poetic composition or the care taken over details of court ceremonial prevail among high-level functionaries over banal duties connected with day-to-day administration. To choose the wrong tone of voice or commit an error of taste might mean compromising one's honor and exposing oneself to reprimand. But it is above all the female universe, captured as if in a constant shadow play, that gives the measure of the subtlety of shades of sentiment and form developed in this period of Japanese history. Morris does an excellent job of rendering this constant search for an "emotional quality," *aware*, characteristic not only of nature or of art, but also of persons and things.

At court, fugitive or more lasting love affairs interweave in a gallant carousel. The women judge the men by the way they rise out of bed in the morning, by their ability to express how overcome they were in their abandonment. Even if immediately afterward both were negotiating another affair with other lovers. This merry-go-round was dominated by a magnificent sense of transience; it was "a floating world," like the interpretation that Heian culture had given to the Buddhism that had reached it from India. The court world was focused on the elegance of clothing, placing the right colors together, pursuing a fragile and perfect architecture. Sentiments, too, were pure elegance at the limit of coldness. This was a world unshaken by the passions, but motivated by a careful search for behavior that would express both preciosity and naturalness. The court was so taken up by its games that for over two centuries the Japanese did not even maintain relations with China, and a functionary felt himself to be severely punished if he was sent to head a province that was not within reach of the court.

As Barbara Carnevali recounts in her *Le apparenze sociali: Per una filosofia del prestigio*, that preoccupation for exterior things was common to other courts and other aristocracies, and it was given epic treatment in Proust's *À la recherche du temps perdu*. For Marcel, the Prince of Guermantes is the model of what he would like to be, but cannot because he does not belong to the social class that still has the true "class" to behave with elegance in every situation, even when obliged to eat in somewhat plebeian places or climb over a divan. It is that immediate quality, that *savoir faire* that the Paris aristocracy represents in daily life, in the art of conversation, in not taking itself too seriously, and in nonetheless being solidly installed in its own manners and in having the "right forms."

Traces of a similar aesthetics of the quotidian can also be found in a tribe as distant from the Paris salons as the Kaguru, a people in central Tanzania studied by Thomas O. Beidelman. (*The Cool Knife: Imagery of Gender, Sexuality and Moral Education in Kaguru Initiation Ritual.*) In Kaguru society, the norms that regulate access to sexuality for the young are accompanied by rites of initiation. The rite for males is circumcision, justified by mythical tales that say that it was a woman who first performed a circumcision on her man because she then enjoyed sex more and she found him more aesthetically more pleasing. Men undergo it because there is in this appreciation of how they look something like a tie that holds together the society to which they belong. The sphere of Kaguru sexuality is connected with both an ethics and an aesthetics of a way to follow if one wants to be an adequate adult.

Something analogous, but this time on the level of local mind, can be found in the Tuareg society that Barbare Fiore has studied for many years, where the categories of womanly beauty are based on the much-loved desert, and the women considered the most beautiful are those whose striae, or stretch marks, most resemble the lines that the wind traces on the dunes.

This habit of ordinary ethics to tend toward aesthetics can be explained by our society's very idea of virtue. We say of a highly skilled violinist that he is a virtuoso and we attribute his skill a craft, an action, and an art that one learns and then forgets; a virtue for which we seem to have no responsibility, unless it is in the merit of having adopted it. That "bravura" has no moral connotation, because in having become a "form" of action it has lost the idea that it involved a choice and an event. Certainly, that skill and know-how is appreciated by all of society because it indicates work and is an example of assiduity, but its quality leaves out of consideration the notion that the virtuoso violinist must also be morally "good." This is what Aristotle thought of the virtues and their not directly ethical nature. The artisan whose hands "know" how to make a suit, a lute, a painting, or a piece of embroidery, is someone who has transformed a day-by-day ethical effort into something that has become apparently obvious and natural. Aesthetics "cools" the passions that lead to a competence, just as it "cools" the motivations by which a society gives itself forms, up to the point of having them appear natural and obvious, as if they had always existed and the question was only how to make them dance and play—a pure question of style. It is as if aesthetics were an ethics in which passions and emotions find a substitute in expertise and in a "sense of measure" that demands a precision without precision—that is, a capacity to use precision playfully.

There is in the tendency of everyday moralities to become aesthetics a clever move on the part of the "device" that contributes to holding society together. Subtract from the idea of moral choice what people do in the details of their own quotidian experience means creating in it, in the space in which they live day by day, the "play" (in the sense of a lock that has a certain amount of play), an elasticity that permits not feeling oneself closed in, but feeling that one's own life has a margin, a magnificent ability to permits oneself a certain relaxation, a certain sense of "taking it easy" with oneself. The sense of a time and a space that are not only connected with the commandment of the necessary and the dutiful. The margin within which individuals and communities can not only follow the forms of life that are given to them, but live them with style, and with their own style. This is what one senses listening to the jokes, the exchange of insults, the mutual teasing in the local dialect of men at the edge of a square or on the seashore in front of the nets. It is what you sense when you listen to women talking about their children and their husbands, judging things that have happened or are happening, telling each other their dreams and offering theories about what they mean. It is the interval that permits daily life to "give out" its savor and that perhaps nothing expresses more fully that humor, irony, and a lightness conquered on a daily basis.

There are some who have used poetry to try to show that aesthetics is the mother of ethics. In the speech he made on receiving the Nobel prize in 1987 Joseph Brodski spoke about this question:

> On the whole, every new aesthetic reality makes man's ethical reality more precise. For aesthetics is the mother of ethics; The categories of "good" and "bad" are, first and foremost, aesthetic ones, at least etymologically preceding the categories of "good" and "evil." If in ethics not "all is permitted," it is precisely because not "all is permitted" in aesthetics, because the number of colors in the spectrum is limited. The tender babe who cries and rejects the stranger or who, on the contrary, reaches out to him, does so instinctively, making an aesthetic choice, not a moral one.

For Brodski, the point is that it is the formal rules of aesthetics, poetry and especially literature that give a different form to daily life, transforming and shaping its repetitions when they become the prey of regimes that use them to perpetuate their own "yester-days" pawned off as tomorrows. As Brodski says:

> The philosophy of the state, its ethics—not to mention its aesthetics—are always "yesterday." Language and literature are always "today," and often—particularly in the case where a political situation is orthodox—they may even constitute "tomorrow." One of literature's merits is precisely that it helps a person to make the time of his existence more specific, to distinguish himself from the crowd of his predecessors as well as his like numbers, to avoid tautology—that is, the fate otherwise known by the honorific term, "victim of history." What makes art in general, and literature in particular, remarkable, what distinguishes them from life, is precisely that they abhor repetition. In everyday life you can tell the same joke thrice and, thrice getting a laugh, become the life of the party. In art, though, this sort of conduct is called "cliché."

Brodski notes that aesthetics is the mother of ethics, following Dostoevski's idea that "beauty will save the world":

> It is precisely in this applied, rather than a Platonic, sense that we should understand Dostoevsky's remark that beauty will save the world, or Matthew Arnold's belief that we shall be saved by poetry. It is probably too late for the world, but for the individual man there always remains a chance. An aesthetic instinct develops in man rather rapidly, for, even without fully realizing who he is and what he actually requires, a person instinctively knows what he doesn't like and what doesn't suit him. In an anthropological respect, let me reiterate, a human being is an aesthetic creature before he is an ethical one.

Therefore, it is not that art, particularly literature, is a byproduct of our species' development, but just the reverse. If what distinguishes us from other members of the animal kingdom is speech, then literature—and poetry in particular, being the highest form of locution—is, to put it bluntly, the goal of our species.

Brodski claims for poetry and literature the role of "preceding" society, and especially of guaranteeing the individuals who make it up the ability of not having to identify with the "already" that came before them and exists around them. "The point is not so much that virtue does not constitute a guarantee for producing a masterpiece, as that evil, especially political evil, is always a bad stylist." This is because "a man with taste, particularly literary taste, is less susceptible to the refrains and the rhythmical incantations peculiar to any version of political demagoguery." Brodski concludes, "The more substantial an individual's aesthetic experience is, the sounder his taste, the sharper his moral focus, the freer—though not necessarily the happier— he is."

In short, aesthetics can be a source of ethics because it can save it from the embalming to which moral and political regimes condemn it, and perhaps also from the simple, habit-driven nature of daily life. Thus poetry as a matrix, as an archaeology of society, as a guarantee that a society not permit itself to become rigid and not stiffen in its forms. The amusing thing is that as a poet, Brodski justifies affirmations by referring to an anthropological interpretation that sees taste and disgust as one of the prime affirmations of the human being.

17
Impertinence

What leads men to be virtuous? Plato raised the question as one of the principal torments of his investigation. How was it possible that a man like Alcibiades, dearer to Socrates than anyone else, educated in the deepest cult of virtue, should then become one of the cleverest bertrayers of his city, sell himself to the Spartans in order to combat his fellow-Athenians, and, as if that were not enough, sell himself to the Persians as well, to the point of ending his life being killed by the Spartans while he was in Persia? Alcibiades was proof that the exercise of virtue does not make us virtuous, and that morality is not only a question of social formation.

Probably Plato wanted to pass on to us that particular Alcibiades precisely because he represents the inexhaustible resources of impertinence, the refusal to succeed and to "conform" either to general behavior or to what was expected of him. Alcibiades represents the flicker of good or evil that enables anyone to give one good kick and separate himself from the herd of the majority that surrounds us. It is an antidote—dangerous in its negative thrust, but still an antidote—to the moral coherence of the bigots and to the good manners and the virtues that can become propriety or doing good in order to appear to be on the side of good. Alcibiades want farther: he was not interested only in seeming good. He was a traitor who, above all, betrayed people's expectations of him and a fixed image of himself. On the other hand, did not his master—his lover and his beloved Socrates—die precisely for that reason? That is, to demonstrate that there is something that goes beyond the laws of Athens? Was he not accused of the greatest infamy, that of not respecting the gods of his city? Socrates died in order to open up the possibility of impertinence, he who had throughout his life created disturbances, annoyed people, and challenged accepted morality with his questions and his behavior.

Ordinary morality has a limitation signaled by someone who shows that there is a way to reach beyond it. The "contrarian," the witness to the exception and to the amoral (according to the majority) but who opens new paths to everyday morality, indicates other possibilities and moves ordinary morality in the direction of a dynamic that seems inappropriate to it but that turns out to be essential to it if it really wants to be vital.

This is not to be confused, however, with those who, especially in our contemporary society, seek success by being immoral and impose their own immorality as current morality. The corrupt or the corrupter is someone who claims that the entire world is as corrupt as he is and that his immorality should become majority behavior. To do so, he needs to publicize his immorality and show it off in public as much as possible.

This has no relation to the courage of "impertinence," the courage to say and to do what the majority does not say or do. The impertinent person does not seek applause, but rather to be the cause of scandal, an obstacle to cowardice, a resistance to the "everything is just fine."

And yet, looking at things from another viewpoint, even the task of the "contrarian" is possible only if there exists a context within which its exceptionality can be relevant.

If we understand why we set about to write this book, we can summarize the reasons in a simple consideration borrowed from Marshall Sahlins. In *The Western Illusion of Human Nature*, Sahlins invites us to stop thinking and believing that we are basically bad and need someone to govern us, control us, and show us the right way. Anthropology teaches us that society, seen as daily life, is capable of producing rules for supporting a healthy reciprocity, but, above all, it tells a second and disconcerting truth, disliked both on the right and on the left, which is that society comes before the state and before reformers and professional revolutionaries (the avant-gardes, alas!).

This means, from our viewpoint, accepting the fact that there is an ethics in the form of a "mutuality of being" (which the anthropologists sometimes call kinship) in which others "become predicates of one's own existence, and vice versa," that is, there is an "integration of certain relationships, hence the participation of certain others in one's own being." Moreover, "if 'I am another,' then the other is also my own purpose." It follows from that observation, according to Sahlins, "neither is experience an exclusively individual function. In the manner and to the extent that people are members of one another, so may experiences be shared among them. Not at the level of sensation, of course, but at the level of meaning: of what it is that happens, which is the human cum communicable experience." This thought links Sahlins to the ordinary ethics of Cavell and to the "local mind" as a combination of experience of and familiarity with a place and a circle of persons. Hence "people suffered illnesses as a result of moral or religious transgressions of their relating – a common ethnographic finding."

That same "mutuality of being," as a given of anthropological experience, saves us from philosophy's stumbles and its rejection of the human. It is related to the *a priori* elements of experience that Maine de Biran spoke of and that were taken up again by the phenomenology dear to Emmanuel Lévinas. It remains in daily life as a "given" that precedes us and within which we are steeped in otherness.

All of that does not found any ethical essentialism, however, nor does it found any new "natural morality," as the neurolinguists and the "facile" affirmations of the neurosciences would have it. There is no biological primacy of morality sculpted into our mirroring neurons: if one source of morality is the mimetic instinct, that instinct can easily turn into its opposite because mimesis, as René Girard has taught us, calmly leads to antagonism and to the homicide— ritual or not—of the other.

In this sense, ordinary ethics offers itself as a cultural possibility—not as a necessity. François Jullien, an acute student of forms of life in China, remands us that a civilization like the Chinese expresses the virtue of "humanity" (*ren*) as a combination of the character for "man" and that for "two," adding that "every virtue of man is in man and manifests itself the minute there are two people." Man is already dual; he is already plurality installed in his singularity.

But, precisely, we are talking about possibility, a virtue that is virtual and that is developed as a virtue of humanity. If that "mutual relationship" is the necessary condition for the existence of an ethics, by itself it does not seem to be sufficient to its manifestation because it presupposes a shared idea of what we call the "other." Because, when we think of how the last century closed and the current one opened (Yugoslavia, Rwanda, Chechnya, etc.), the problem is still and always will be what can happen when in the relationship between two "entities" the two are treated, for one reason or another, with differing valences. This is the revenge of a facile admission of cultural difference; the vendetta of a much-acclaimed multiculturalism that cuts off at the root the possibility that, beyond difference, the other may be me.

From the viewpoint of anthropology, there is something disturbing here. Very well, "culture is the human nature," as Marshall Sahlins tells us, putting us on guard against any new naturalism that might come from the neo-Thomists or from the neuroscience laboratories. Certainly, we are social beings. But for precisely those reasons we should always remember that every relationship can at a certain moment be broken, explode, or throw reciprocity into a crisis, with the terrible consequences that we know all too well, and—always "culturally"—lead us to destroying our neighbor. Luckily for us, this is obviously not a fact of nature, but do we know how to sustain—in the literal sense of holding up, carrying over our heads—that is one of the ways in which "a form of meaning" can be realized?

This is where Plato's dilemma about Alcibiades begins, but it is also where the profound key to ordinary ethics begins, the key to why ethics does not escape the radical question of possibility and liberty. "The mutuality of being" does not exclude Alcibiades and his betrayals, and it does not exclude liberty. It does not exclude the inexplicable movement by which every history, every individual destiny, jeopardizes, as if for the first time, the fortunate and fatal, terrible and fantastic relation between our belonging to the populated daily world and the part of ourselves that remains withdrawn from it. ▪

Also available from Prickly Paradigm Press:

continued